AT THE HANDS OF MEN

Edited by

Natalie Nightingale

First published in Great Britain in 2002 by
POETRY NOW
Remus House,
Coltsfoot Drive,
Peterborough, PE2 9JX
Telephone (01733) 898101
Fax (01733) 313524

All Rights Reserved

Copyright Contributors 2002

HB ISBN 0 75434 363 4
SB ISBN 0 75434 364 2

FOREWORD

Although we are a nation of poets we are accused of not reading poetry, or buying poetry books. After many years of listening to the incessant gripes of poetry publishers, I can only assume that the books they publish, in general, are books that most people do not want to read.

Poetry should not be obscure, introverted, and as cryptic as a crossword puzzle: it is the poet's duty to reach out and embrace the world.

The world owes the poet nothing and we should not be expected to dig and delve into a rambling discourse searching for some inner meaning.

The reason we write poetry (and almost all of us do) is because we want to communicate: an ideal; an idea; or a specific feeling. Poetry is as essential in communication, as a letter; a radio; a telephone, and the main criterion for selecting the poems in this anthology is very simple: they communicate.

CONTENTS

Title	Author	Page
What Changes?	Jonis Pastit	1
Responsibility	Kathleen Potter	2
The Crossing	Dorothy Buyers	3
Love And Peace	Reuben Bilton	4
War-Torn Afghanistan	Vivienne Joyce	5
A Lifetime Of Hatred	Efrosyni Hobbs	6
Flags And Graffiti	Natalie Watton	7
Miracles Out Of Ruins	Don Okoko	8
A Soldier's Epitaph	Thérèse Fisher	9
War And Peace	Sonia Richards	10
The Jewess	Mariegold Heron	10
Dearest One	S Yates	11
The Battle	Yvonne Friend	12
The Irish Fight	Patricia Orton	12
To Autumn: The Fallen	Martha Watson Brown	13
Carrion Eaters Peck And Gnaw . . .	Robin Colville	14
The Holy Land	Steve Glason	14
Chechnya	M Booth	15
EGM's Peace Agenda	Edward Graham Macfarlane	16
War And Peace	Ann	17
A Night To Remember	Janet Cavill	18
Landscape Forecasting The Falklands War	Ali Cohen	18
Death : Incidental	Lee Catherine Simpson	19
Tragedy	Pauline Hales	20
Peace Not War	Alma Montgomery Frank	20
War And Peace	Carole Mitchell	21
In The Name Of Love	Freda Grieve	21
When Will It End?	Eduardo del Rio Escalona	22
The Ardennes - July 1944	Thelma Kellgren	23
Dunkirk - The Final Tribute	A Yap-Morris	24
The Silent Revolution	Vina Curren	25
Thoughts On The Troubles In Ireland	Edward Farren	26
Is Faith Religion Or Obsession?	Sheila M Storr	27

It Was Just the War	S V Batten	28
Souls Of Soldiers	Tracy Mitchell	29
Suburbia	Joan R Gilmour	29
Violent Ulster	Alan Moore	30
New York September 11 2001	M Elizabeth Workman	31
War And Peace	T Lawrence	32
Blasphemy	Olga Allen	33
Time To Get It Right	Richard J Bradshaw	34
On The Longest Day	Anna Taylor	34
My Thoughts Of The World Today	Peter Antonian	35
Five Bells	T P Coggins	35
Front Line	Byron McAlpine	36
The Changing Face Of Conflict	Di Bagshawe	37
Honour Your Mother	D J Price	38
Bang!	Bryan Davies	39
War	Shane Stephens	40
No Savoir	Tali Rose	41
Repent	Bill Williams	42
The Skirmish	Joy M Bufton	43
Peace, Peace, But There Is No Peace	Douglas Charing	44
Omagh Staccato	Marylee Rounce	44
1914-1918	Godfrey Dodds	45
The Armour Of God	R Baker	46
The Aftermath	Margaret A P Quinn	47
The Soldier's Last Words	Garry Knowles	48
Again And Again	Derek Blackburn	48
Darkness Of Our Age	Lyndon Thomas	49
How Do We Tell The Children?	Leslie F Higgins	50
No One Remembers The Heroes	Damien Aked	51
Israel	Phillip A Taylor	52
Baby Blues	Kathryn Bocking	52
Qualquilia	Charles Webster	53
The Peace Rose	U Johnson	53
War And Peace	Norman Bissett	54
Sigh Today As Woman Becomes Veg	Robert Harrison	55

Love And Peace	Brigid O'Donnell	56
A Game Of Hearts	Lucy E Lutzke	56
Hear . . . O Israel	Lew Park	57
The Terrorist	Mary Cole	57
I Am You We Are They	John Marshall	58
Hope	M Andrews	58
Just A Thought	Deborah Foley	59
No Peace On Earth	F Hodgkinson	60
Bethlehem 2002	Alix Brown	61
Another Hand	Bob White	62
Lost Property	Jules A Riley	62
Terrorist	J Stenning	63
A Schoolchild At War	Thomas Harrison	64
War	John Edney	65
Kabul Women	Julie Longman	66
Untitled	Catherine Fleming	66
The Poor Bugger	Leslie Loader	67
It's Gonna Explode	Charles Darkly	68
The Road To Peace With Afghanistan In Mind	Mary Ferguson	68
Peace Not War!	Nicholas Maughan	69
The Duel	Mary Ratcliffe	70
Omagh	Angela Walder	71
Insanity	Stephanie Harness	72
Blitzed	Sigrid Armitage	72
War And Peace	Sharon Ferguson	73
Borderline	Linda P Brookes	74
What Is Peace?	Caroline Pybus	75
Red In Contrast	Margaret Heavenor	76
Osama bin Laden	Margaret Lightbody	77
Why?	Hilary Barton	78
Shalom - Salem	Linda Levy	78
War And Peace	Josephine Marks	79
Battlefields	David Evans	79
A Land Fit For Heroes	Aled Hughes	80
11 September 2001	Maria-Christina	81
All Quiet On The Cemetery Front	Ian D Henery	82

The Children	Frederick Seymour	83
Tribute	Liam Fyffe	84
Peace	M Gibson	85
Conflict	Tilla B Smith	86
Somewhere A Candle Glows	Lorna Troop	86
Message For 2001	E Kronbergs	87
War (Part 2)	Corwin Barber	88
Aftermath Africa	Joan Briggs	88
Newsflash	J M Rosson Gaskin	89
A Night In The Life	Greig Hepson	90
September Morn	Ruth Terry	91
The Telegram	Diane Berthelot	92
War And Peace	Karen Disney	92
War Child	Stephen Hibbeler	93
Why?	Angela Burse	93
Just A Dream	Roy Dickinson	94
War	Henry Disney	95
War And Peace	James Stephen Cameron	96
War And Peace	Susanne Semmence	97
War	R S Hooper	98
World Conflicts	R D Hiscoke	99
Rise Up	Chris Ward	100
Farewell To Arms	Bernard Brown	100
War And Peace	Jean McGovern	101
War And Peace	B Mitchell	102
Peace In Northern Ireland	J L Preston	103
What Peace?	Norman Chandler	104
War And Peace	N Rudge	104
Only News	Michelle Landon	105
Testosterone	Lesley S Robinson	106
The Power Of The World	E A Triggs	106
War And Peace	Janet Marie Lord	107
11th Of September	Mollie D Earl	108
Love Thy Neighbour	Barrington Delevante	109
Bravehearts	Allan Wood	110
War And Peace	Carol Sherwood	111
Step Back From The Brink	Welch Jeyaraj Balsingam	112
The Button	Bert Booley	113

Title	Author	Page
War	Siôn Griffiths	114
Innocent Victims	Sophie Trenchard	114
How Many Hands Rock The Cradle?	Tim Frogman	115
The Snows Are Still Melting	WJFH	116
War And Peace	Eileen Kyriacou	117
The Anguish Lives On	Eve McGrath	118
Enter The Dragon	Margaret Whyte	119
Away With It	Clare Marie Zeidrah Keirrissia Marshall	120
War	Lin Bourne	121
Absent Hearts	F Cooper	122
A Century Of Shame	Albert Brindle	122
No More War - I Pray To God	Ian Deal	123
The Things One Says	Celia M Paulo	124
Athena And Pegasus	Ann Copland	125
The Misery Of War	Margaret Warkup	126
Inhumanity	John E Lindsay	126
Babi Yar	John Clancy	127
Lament For A Date Of Birth: The Sacking Of Berlin	Rebecca Darley	128
Greystoke	Winnie Pat Lee	129
Silent Tears In Omagh Peace On Earth, Goodwill . . .	Iris Day	130
Confusion	Eileen M Pratt	131
The Poppy	Jean Greenall	132
Asylum Seekers	Emelie Buckner	132
Fragments Of War	Luisa Allan	133
Game Over	Marilyn Hodgson	134
Ulster Night Out	Jane Bagnall	135
After The Bomb	F Macdonald	136
Battleground	Jonathan Pegg	137
Balkans	A C Dancer	138
While You Still Have Time	Ted Harriott	140
Optimist In Residence	Allan Bula	141
Vietnam 1965 - A Peasant's Plea	Angela Cheyne	142
Holiday Camp?	Margo Biggs	142
Serre Road British Cemetery	Bob Proud	143

War	William Allan	144
A Prisoner	Derek Webster	145
Recipes For War	Joyce Atkinson	146
September 11th 2001	Susan Skinner	147
Israel	F Dyke	148
Earth's Hope	Joyce Coghlan	148
September 11th	Mark Allibon	149
Way Of Life	Mary Neill	150
Exodus	Elizabeth Brewer	151
Why?	Gordon J Hellier	152
Holy War	Carol Glover	153

WHAT CHANGES?

A history of blood and tears, death and vengeance through the years
The Holocaust, Nazis, death and pain then build an Israel start again
Bomb the British, clear the way, steal Arab land and build to stay
Push Palestinians to the wall, suicide bombers heed the call
Maim and kill the old and young, purge them from land
                                        where they belong
The death toll mounts by bomb and bullet but Israel's
                                        might will see her through it
Supported by the USA where financial arguments hold sway
No going back Israel will last - this time a Palestinian Holocaust

Orange walks and Orange Men - nationalists all dressed in green
Kill and maim, bomb and blast a fragile peace not meant to last
Bigots abound on every side - nowhere to go, nowhere to hide
Apologise for what you've done, massacres, killings, losing a son
Catholics, Protestants do you really care just an answer
                                        to a simple prayer
Look in the mirror what do you see? Orange and green the choice is free
With your history, looking back, why not a nation dressed in black
Stupid messages, religious taunts for a piece of land nobody wants

Vietnam, Somalia, the Bay of Pigs never friends while Castro lives
Defeated but a chance to create pain, Iraq, the Afghans, Iraq again
The Twin Towers, nobody asked just why, death descended
                                        from the sky
History of no understanding of smaller nations, less demanding
World domination based on greed not connected to basic need
Financial scandals rule today let's make them look the other way
Divert attention what would they like another so called
                                        pre-emptive strike?
Does it matter where we use our force to overcome this discourse?
Cry you mothers, bring out your dead, media and
                                        politicians must be fed.

Jonis Pastit

RESPONSIBILITY

First world technology bringing
    into our homes famine and blight.
Revealing such stark naked pain
    wretched Third World peoples in flight.
Mid comfort, we avert our eyes
    squeamish witnesses to the sight
Of their silent acquiescence
    amid the horrors of their plight.
Like the Christ who was crucified
    they don't question their lot despite
Infants suckling at empty breasts,
    luminous eyes seared by fright.
This the ultimate betrayal
    by politicians too polite.
Obscuring human misery
    better their cause to expedite
Control over corrupt leaders
    abusers of power and might,
Who let populations wither
    vanquished by resources finite.
God forgive our indecision
    time for First World to unite
Show a spark of humanity
    help our brothers to see the light.
Culpable of war by omission
    it's our turn to take up the fight.

Kathleen Potter

THE CROSSING

The men were murdered in a field
Outside the town, some forty shot
Without a trial, killed in cold blood
And buried in a trench.

They were driven to their death by coach
Through empty city streets at night;
We saw the coach on TV news
Approach a zebra crossing.

Had town officials once conferred
About that crossing and agreed
Where it should be and on which day
The stripes be painted white?

Then citizens could cross the road
Pavement to pavement, east to west,
In safety between halting cars
That headed north or south.

The coach of death moved steadily
Over the crossing on its way
To unmarked country lanes beyond
The city and its laws.

If on that night a man had stepped
On to that crossing, would the man
Who drove that coach have used his brakes
And stopped to let him pass?

Dorothy Buyers

LOVE AND PEACE

Love is the mystical force that binds all together,
love is the light and love is the saviour of us all.
Love is creation, the awe and wonder it inspires,
love is creation and everything within.
Love is all animals, all creatures great and small.
Love and peace is a gift to us all, to be found in every heart.
Love for your fellow man and woman,
love for all, for are we all not brothers?
Show your love for your fellow man,
let your every action be full of love,
let us live in peace and harmony,
let us live as one, under the law of love.
Forgive your enemy, shower him or her with love,
a wise man makes friends not enemies,
for it is better to be wise and full of love,
than to be full of hatred and without compassion for your brothers.
Give up your hatred, repent,
open your heart to peace, love and understanding.
Look towards the light and let your heart bathe in love,
for love is the beginning, the ending and everything in-between.
Love your brothers and sisters, regardless if they are short or tall,
thin or fat, ugly or beautiful, show all love and goodwill,
love your enemies ten fold, love those who want to fight you,
throw only flowers at them and love, for love shall conquer all,
and those who hurt you and do you evil, show them love,
show them the way, the path of love and if you can't convert them,
show them no malice, give them no pain, love them all the more,
for they are the ones who need more loving.
Feel the love in your heart, revel in the sensation,
share the love and goodwill with all you meet, spread the love,
for it is contagious, love cannot be stopped, for it is the law.
Never stop loving, no matter how hard love hurts,
do not become disheartened because love is as prolific as the herb,
 it belongs to us all, love is within all our hearts,
feel it for all things, feel love with every beat, take it with you,

smile to all, the smile of love, share your possessions,
share your food, share your clothes and share your love.
Love all, love strong for love is good, love is the light,
love is the eternal gift of the creator, love, love, love,
for love is the righteous path, the path of love can be followed by all,
the first step on this path is to find the love in your heart,
it is not hidden, for love cannot hide, forgive people their mistakes,
forget all your petty squabbles, for love is bigger than any one man,
bigger than any one situation, bigger than us all,
and if we love hard enough, it shall save us all,
and remember, if you love something, let it roam free,
if it doesn't return it wasn't meant to be,
but let this not blind you to the power of love,
for love is the power and the glory, love everyone,
have love for all, like a mother loves her children,
and as the Buddha said, see everyone as your mother.
Have love in your eyes and in your heart,
love with all of your heart, for love is why we are all here.
Love is what makes the world go round, let us all love one another,
and may peace and love be with you always.

Reuben Bilton

WAR-TORN AFGHANISTAN

A mother weeps, for death's cold hand
Has touched the child who starved with hunger at her empty breast,
An old man, bent with years and frail
Finds strength to lift his dear wife's body to its yawning grave.
Young orphans, desolate, shivering, sad,
Shed anguished tears as grey despair shrouds all they ever knew
Whilst those well blessed are discontent
And dare complain their blessings aren't enough and they want more.
These suffering innocents expose
The shameful selfishness and greed which tarnishes some souls.

Vivienne Joyce

A Lifetime Of Hatred

Babes born to the sound
of infernal, unstoppable guns
I weep for the legacy
of hatred you inherit.

Children running a gauntlet
amid bigotry and aggression
born of centuries-old conflicts
I mourn your future.

Young men and women cut
down in your prime,
sacrificed and martyred
in blood-soaked lands.

The bloodstained hands
of adults weaned and reared
to perpetuate loathing and war
wreak a vengeance that escalates.

Not many left to die
of old age, a natural death;
mothers, fathers, seasoned in battle
bury their children with pride.

If only compassion
could take the place of pride
if only peace
mattered more than war.

I shed tears for you all,
lives lived in hatred
yet the violence won't stop
until you weep for each other.

Efrosyni Hobbs

FLAGS AND GRAFFITI

With bottles and stones
They let out their anger
With bricks and bullets
They fight for their 'cause'

With flags and graffiti
They sound out their fury
With tongues edged as daggers
They shout out their jeers

When bricks hit my garden
I look at dead roses
When flames hit my car
I just want to hide

But this is my home
I've been here forever
And here with my friends
We'll stand side by side

With grills on my window
I watch the scenes nightly
With bars on my door
I sit here and cry

With hope in my heart
I pray for its ending
With love in my heart
I pray Lord - some day.

Natalie Watton

MIRACLES OUT OF RUINS

There wouldn't be any need for life or sense of purpose
Nor would there be any creation without sense of purpose
But irony of life; mankind mocks creation and its purpose
Upshot came the trial of the creation and its purpose, but
Out of His mercy we find there're miracles out of ruins.

There was the big bang when it blasted, as was the beginning,
Enthusiasts claimed not to have witnessed it in that beginning,
Save to say evolution was to blame for our failures, of course
Our failures indeed to protect our environs the gifts of nature,
As all mankind black and white evolved from one genealogy.

Is theirs religion, think of Afghanistan as troubled waters?
Theirs is not of religious cleansing but of tribal sentiments.
Pause for Israelis and Palestine is theirs religious conflict?
The house divide; where are world leaders the world's silent
World conflict; biblical or not there're miracles out of ruins.

On top of the flooding trees a child is born
Of the Mozambique River's tide and floods.
Oh! Of collapsed buildings lives are pulled
On September 11 of Trade Centre of New York.
In time of peace and war there're miracles out of ruins.

There are peaceful minds where the rivers glow
Northern Ireland inhabitants long for peace not of war,
'Cause there're nothing in names but what you make of them
Catholic and Protestants are Christians and only one mighty God
Courage forgive courage reign and there're miracles out of ruins.

In world of anarchy lawlessness rules streets and cities unperturbed
Save rhetoric, I see no truce or new world order this century reign,
But evidence of poverty and rumours of war and refugees everywhere!
The moon man landed but none created Earth save defile
                                            peaceful world
Upshot dust for dust but there're miracles out of ruins.

Don Okoko

A Soldier's Epitaph

I never dreamt 'twould be like this, or I'd have feared the thought
of war,
And I'd have dread and not been thrilled by the enemy's battle roar,
Shaking are my hands - dead men lie around my feet,
No coffin for them to lie in - no snow-white shrouding sheet,
No glorious funeral, though their deaths were brave,
By brave men wrought, who were death's slave.
I killed a man last night, and I watched as he died,
The pain in his eyes as he whimpered and writhed.
I know that I killed many others, unseen behind the trees,
But I didn't see their eyes, as they too sank to their knees.

Now, as the sun sets on this, my last day in this world,
As night sees the battle's end with no victorious flags unfurled,
Around me I gaze, feel the hurt and the pain,
Remember comrades I've lost, pray they've not died in vain,
That somehow from out all the fears and the tears,
Will surface the peace that we've lost through the years.
The light is fading fast, and I can scarcely see to write,
I don't care that I'm not keeping watch, I've lost the will to fight.

It's so quiet now - but what was that - a movement behind that tree!
How strange - I cannot feel a thing - didn't hear a sound but the
bullet sing.
Dear God, I'm so sorry for all the lives I've taken,
How could I have been so easily led - so foolishly mistaken,
Please take care of those I've loved, my five and 20 years,
Make them happy once again - mend their hearts and dry their tears,
I'm tired - I'm so cold - now I'll never grow old.
Goodbye sweet life - farewell my wife,
Look after our children three
And remember me - remember me.

Thérèse Fisher

WAR AND PEACE

Since time began
Man has fought to conquer
His neighbours and acquire
New land.

Greed and power urged
Him on to commit
Acts of atrocity - all morals
Purged.

Small groups of protesters
For justice and revenge
Whistling in the wind
While hatred festers.

Can 'Armageddon' be far behind
While man pushes forward
Such inequality - destruction
Such uncomprehending humankind.

Sonia Richards

THE JEWESS

I saw my mother in a dream,
blown up in size
and with a masculine mien - as though
to include her domination.
This Irish house stays firm
surrounded by gale force winds.

I lodge here while studying
and accept Catholic welcome,
but as strong a force as the winds
is more news of Israeli revenge.
(The Beatitudes
grow from Leviticus,

love being known before Christ).
The dream conveyed I should
revere my mother and speak well of her
in spite of her cold expression
she had wit and dignity
and belonged to a suffering race.

Mariegold Heron

DEAREST ONE

What is this I hold in my hand?
This price of clay from a foreign land,
Before this lovely day is done,
This earth that is bathed in the warmth of the sun,
May cover me with this self-same clay,
And hide me from the light of day.

Dear Lord, don't let it start again,
This hissing steel that falls like rain,
Upon this earth that now lies still, will cut and maim
And try to kill my comrades who are with me now.
Dearest I only wish you were here
To take away this awful fear.

I reach out but you're not there,
I turn my head to see,
The ghostly stumps of trees
That were so splendid in the summer air.
This wood that heard the bluebells ring,
And saw the skylark rise to sing.

Please don't forget me in your thoughts
Or in your everlasting dreams.

Goodbye my love.

S Yates

THE BATTLE

Three in the morning, I can't close my eyes
There's a battle raging in my head
The clock ticks on and on
But the battle in my head just keeps going.

Canons and explosions in my head and before my eyes
Flashes of coloured lights all around
The hands on the clock move steadily on
Now it's nearing four in the morning.

Counting the minutes to melt down
Get up and walk around
Tears are flowing, so much pain
And the battle rages on.

What did I do to deserve this pain?
Surely I'm not that bad a person
Please make the clock go faster
I need to take that pain relief.

Migraine, the worst battle to fight
It takes over your whole body and mind
Steadily, as the dawn is breaking
So tired, sleep comes and the battle subsides.

Yvonne Friend

THE IRISH FIGHT

Our squaddies, as you call them
Target the murderous beasts
Who target innocent people
For the sake of political beliefs.

How many squaddies have these terrorists killed?
Not many, cos the squaddies fight back!
But they've killed and maimed by the hundred
Innocents who can't fight back.

They'll blow the limbs off children
And leave them crippled for life;
Tar and feather a woman
For being a Protestant wife!

All this terrorist violence
Is just a weak excuse
For those who want to hurt and hate
To have their evil way.

Patricia Orton

TO AUTUMN: THE FALLEN

The leaves, crispy and fallen, unmortal, dead.
Wave goodbye, shake their heads: 'Farewell autumn', no more said.
Brief is the autumn, colours weep, maples red.

Whiskery branches, shake down leaves onto cold-chilled resting beds,
Autumnal chills fill the air, a voice whispers: 'Winter! Soon be here!'
The leaves, crispy and fallen, unmortal, dead.

Bare-backed trees shiver still as in deepest, darkest, doomed dread;
Frost attack! Fogs found! Cov'ring bark now, still the sound!
Brief is the autumn, colours weep, maples red.

Death knells of high-piled leaves where one treads,
So lonely, they are forgone, forsaken, blown away.
The leaves, crispy and fallen, unmortal, dead.

Spring, summer growth, sun-ray fed,
Once a bud, bright with green blossoming life
One proud in seasons, limp, barren life;
The leaves, crispy and fallen, unmortal, dead.
Brief is the autumn, colours weep, maples red.

Martha Watson Brown

CARRION EATERS PECK AND GNAW...

Carrion eaters peck and gnaw
on flesh putrid with decay
an odour of corruption
hangs heavy as a rolling fog.

The ploughman raises a furrow
of rich red loam
a land made fertile of cadaverous matter
the mould-board carves rank on rank.

I remember a time, now seeming so distant,
before the sarcophagous beast
was loosened from that underworld
when dark brooding had not yet turned
to the cavern of 1,000 mirrors
in each reflections only of the beast
configured in deceit by 1,000 guises.

Armed encampments sit astride the border
hostilities, but a wayward glance, withheld
negotiations for peace, hesitant and protracted
the furrow may yet beget a harvest.

Robin Colville

THE HOLY LAND

Near Israel's holy, sacred shrines
Bullet, gun and rocket whines
Bombers strike in crowded street
(Secretly in huddles meet)

Revenge in form of massive tank
(Gaza City - Western Bank)
Palestinians - not content
Seething anger is their bent.

What is the outcome? I don't know
Warring factions on the go
Peace in tatters - it's a shame
Politicians keen to blame.

Terrorists will always act
Sadly an unpleasant fact
Be on our guard and take a stand
Will calm return to Holy Land?

Steve Glason

CHECHNYA

Cities bombed bulldozed to the sodden ground
Skeleton buildings with flapping doors and mounds
Covering dismembered bodies that rejuvenate scorched earth
Hounded out fleeing humans from their land of birth

A child lies still in cold terrified dread
Too scared to move and a day since fed
Amidst family inert in bludgeoned apathy
A Nato soldier cuddles her in sympathy

Futures blotted out in one foul swoop
Survivors huddled in a border coop
Nato soldiers curse and do what they sent to do
Some grit their teeth as they can only save a few

Russia promised to rebuild the cities.
Move on as history repeats it's a pity
Grosney Palace once splendid, a great delight
Now symbolises defeat, lives lost in a senseless fight

Like chickens cooped, distressed in sodden border tents
Their future without loved ones is viewed with contempt.
Some lucky brethren have found asylum in distant lands
Others wait, yes they wait to return to their motherland.

M Booth

EGM's Peace Agenda

Let the politicians make me first a single global nation.
Merge the nations to end a world of sovereign warring gangs.
It means the global imposition of a democratic world
                                       parliament to rule,
Which means that every child now born will become a
                                       global social tool.
This is what really happened within the USA.
Where all kids are being USA brainwashed every single living day.
Brain-washing has been tested and it works very well,
Bill Clinton is a product and although it is wrong it functions well.
It all depends the kind of message that it is used to drill,
The brains of all the children will demonstrate it will fulfil
The intention of the teachers who apply the theory.
If Globalists are wanted this is the task then that will be the skill.
The general aim will be a world nation to rule over all
                                       world social things.
Much the same (but not exactly) as the scheme to which the US clings
The USA brain-washing is designed for USA (USA loyalty for all)
But the global scheme is bigger thinking (world-wide
                                       democracy is the call)
The new nation is achievable and also the most important way to go.
If peace for mankind is the goal in sight as I hope you will know.
We must reject a world of nations with each nation armed for war.
That's a recipe for more bloodshed which we must not be wishing for.
We must agree that human union is a good thing for us all.
The people of the planet Earth being aimed to steer the universe.
All religions are effete now for not one of the gods are real,
From Zeus to Jehovah - all have lost their political appeal,
All prayers are delusion and this really why.
We need a great global reformation before we are doomed to die,
We must banish all imperialisms and monarchies as well,
There is no need for the upper classes us a story we must tell.
I see only 'homo sapiens' around the world today,
And we can't approve of fascisms with Adolf and
                                       Joseph Stalin gone away.

We need a world suitable for all sorts of people living on Earth now.
And egality for all seems fair to me and my mind anyhow.
I do not propose that gorillas or other apes should join
                                the human throng,
My plan is just for scientific humans willing to join a human singalong.
We may have to kill some revels for the Macfarlane peace plan.
But I am sure we can agree a political loyalty statement for
                                'our people' man!

Edward Graham Macfarlane

WAR AND PEACE

War rages - within.
Barbecue time again.
Smoke drifts in windows;
Music blares out;
Shrieks of laughter;
Cars parked outside.

War rages - within.

How long will this last?
How many more 'do's?'
Shutting doors,
Shutting windows,
Doesn't keep out the noise
That rattles within *me*.

My inner self cries out -
Why was I not invited?
Then *peace* as I acknowledge
My jealousy.
And that most of the *war*
Comes from within *me*!

Ann

A Night To Remember

'If we have to go then we will go together.'
My father uttered these words in the spring of 1942.
He lifted me into the bed, he and my mother shared.
I was six years old and their only child.

War raged over not only Europe, but over most of the world.
Men were being killed, women and children were being killed.
Death may have come as a merciful release
To people held in degrading prison conditions.

They had no one to care for them.
No medicine, little food, no comforts.

When will man ever learn?

I remember that night so well.
Bombs were dropping in the land.
Buildings destroyed
Lives lost, what terrible suffering.

'If we have to go we will go together.'
Those words still ring in my mind.
We lived to see another day.
A day for which we all gave thanks.

When will we ever learn?

Janet Cavill

Landscape Forecasting The Falklands War

January, hammered metal, now
Melts to milky February
As the mild-mannered sun gently stirs
Clouds in whirls of cream.

Jet streams cross each other,
Form a white edged triangle,
Complete with sudden black MRCA
And hex the innocence of field and hedge.

Ali Cohen

DEATH: INCIDENTAL

Soul searching comes with age
we regret more with the passage of time
I believed so much in our cause
death was an integral part of the struggle
but her eyes, her piercing black eyes
haunt me still in my slumber.
I was part of a team, so brave and revered
we stormed her village, her home, her land
and made them pay the price for indifference.
As I put the gun to the man's head, she cried,
I turned and sneered before pulling the trigger
and her father fell.
She stared at me - eyes searching for truths
the implications of her gaze naked - for all to see.
My comrade grabbed her by the hair
his gun resting on her tear-stained cheek.
The trigger was poised for action
and yet she sought more answers from me
a lone soldier in a quest for answers of my own.
With a silent shot, she was gone
another ghostly tribute to the 'triumphs' of war.
As she lay still in the dust, her eyes searched in vain
for a window to my tortured soul.

Lee Catherine Simpson

TRAGEDY

We lunched at the familiar pub
In the sleepy Welsh village.
The planned walk along the infant Wye
Was curtailed by heavy rain,
The tiny church was open,
Elderly ladies were flower arranging,
So we entered through the heavy doors.
On a stone pillar was set a plaque
Commemorating the dead
From the First World War.
We counted the names - 96!
An entire generation had been wiped out
On the French battlefields,
Husbands, sons, brothers killed,
Never to return to their farms and homesteads.
Now other villages in distant lands
Suffer the same catastrophic tragedy.
Young men give their lives for half understood causes.
Has the human race learned nothing
Over the intervening years?

Pauline Hales

PEACE NOT WAR

Peace can prevail in spite of war
When love is just around the corner
War can be prevented if those in power stop to think
Negotiation is far better than weapons
To use, sit round a table and talk
Until a solution has been approved
Then rejoice, thank God for diplomacy
And peace not war will be the reward.

Alma Montgomery Frank

WAR AND PEACE

Never content with what we have
Always wanting more
What can we buy next?
So more money please!
Someone's son is shot in battle
Someone's daughter is blown to bits
So more money please!
What can money do now?
The irreplaceable is lost
Never to return
So more money please!
I think not!
Open your heart, gaze into your enemy's eyes,
Befriend him.
No more money please!
No more weapons to buy.

Carole Mitchell

IN THE NAME OF LOVE

Create peace not war
United in a common purpose
An end to killing and strife,
High toll of human misery
Father with small son
Carries a gun
And child protected
Creeps behind his back
Sniper kills and puts
A boy in his grave.
God's son came down to
Save mankind
In the name of love.

Freda Grieve

WHEN WILL IT END?

There is an abysmal confusion and my soul falls down into it
The so called Muslims; the so called Christians, the Hindus, the Jews!
Are gathering to 'condemn' piously concealing their plot . . .
For more wars and revenge!

I shut my eyes to the horror of satellite pictures . . .
But, as if in a giant web I'm caught in them
I shut my ears to the broadcasts, the lament, the wailing, the mourning!
But the sound of sirens follows me through my sleep

I shut out my trust to the words of nations' leaders and orators
And anyone who rules and preaches, shielded behind their prizes
Silver stars, golden medals, iron crosses, purple hearts . . .
'Proudly won in wars' . . . flushing, on their inflated chests

Who do you think is conquering today in vessels of rancour and death
Who do you think is quenching his thirst with our fears and pain?
Who is ignoring all that blood of helpless mothers and children
Who do you think is mastering our greed in disguises?
Who could be making us slaves, through the vendetta that reigns
Who, but the fallen angel of darkness
Claiming his kingdom amongst us, 'Feasting', from our
                                      mind-twisted ways

He laughs . . .
At our frowning semblance, as if we were in real distress
At the poppies in our lapels in memorial for the deaths
What about the ones, we keep on killing every day?

What a pitiful controversy, we'll all end-up in his claws
As he laughs again and again, feeding from our hypocrisy
And mutants that do our jobs . . . 'amused', by our weakened beliefs
Split in playgrounds of war, while we make out we believe . . .
'That we walk with God alone'

So, why do we speak about Him! If our words are not met
Why do we hide behind His name diving him without respect!
Oh, when will it be the day that we'll stop this masquerade,
Let's get hold of the truth brothers and sisters . . .
Before it is too late'.

Eduardo del Rio Escalona

THE ARDENNES - JULY 1944

It was not really a quarrel,
More a contest of wills.
He gasping, in pain, in German.
I tired, frustrated, in English.
The tent was full of wounded.
For the third time I put
The needle back in his arm.
Why did he rip it out repeatedly?
I had hardly turned away when
I heard his distressed breath;
Yet again with his one good arm
He had pulled off the oxygen.
I put the mask back.
I railed at him like
An old fish wife.
He cowered and
I took his hand.
I was determined he would not die.
I did not know
He was frightened of me.
He had been told that
I would kill him.
I won't - please God, help us.

Thelma Kellgren

DUNKIRK - THE FINAL TRIBUTE

Little ships at bay, listen to what they say
Veterans of long gone war returned to Dunkirk today
From Britain's welcoming shores, commemorating
The bravery of 400,000 soldiering men
Who showed great courage then.

With inborn determination and pride in their country,
Confidence in their leaders, who like Churchill helped
                    make Britain 'great'
Rulers of might and steel - in full command!
They soldiered on into the night in defence of what is good, is right
Then came the timely call to retreat,
Strength in wane, but God renewed that strength
With just minutes to spare, they lined the shores of Dunkirk.

Fleeing silently in disciplined hordes
To little ships anxiously lining the shore.
Poignant memories of the hour that herald dawn
Captured in this final tribute, from grateful men.
Humble and unassuming men who felt, 'it was the call of duty',
Who spoke with pride of a job 'well done'
And who now show gratitude to those who gave their lives,
Stayed behind to proudly serve their country to the end
One last stand to rid the world of Hitler's tyranny.

For though sixty years have gone past, recalling days of tiredness
And hope in reaching Britain's friendly shores.
Thought of anxiously awaiting family and of friends.
Of those who stood in their defence, gave up their lives
                    in hail of German shells.
Yet as they celebrate, more plans were made today
To continue coming to this shore to honour of those
                    brave comrades who are no more.

60 years have passed since the Normandy/Dunkirk crossing. Veterans have decided not to celebrate in so grand a style, because of the ages of the men, but to make individual trips to Dunkirk till they are no longer able.

A Yap-Morris

THE SILENT REVOLUTION

I am you - you are me,
We are one in spirit.
We may not look alike, we may not speak alike
But we feel, we love, we suffer alike - in spirit.

> Oh, for a change of heart
> To kneel together, feel together
> The needs of human kind.

Oh, for a silent revolution.

> If no manna falls from heaven then -
> Earth must provide leaven
> And love and milk of human kindness.

Priests and politicians pontificate
Too soon - it is too late.

Oh, for a silent revolution.

> A quiet miracle, a change of heart.
> Only when we feel deeply, bow our heads humbly,
> Give generously,
> Only then will we witness the quiet miracle -

The silent revolution, a rebirth,
> A new heaven and a new Earth.

Vina Curren

THOUGHTS ON THE TROUBLES IN IRELAND

O pleasant land of Erin,
From whence my forefathers came,
I grieve to see thy sorrow,
Thy tears, thy woes, thy shame;
Thy native sons and daughters
Their life from thee begun,
Are crushing out that very life
With bullet, bomb and gun.
In Ulster's troubled province,
Where sainted Patrick trod
And brought to thee the steadfast faith
In one, true, living God,
Sees brother against brother
Set in enmity and hate,
Whilst thou, their loving mother
Canonly hope and wait
For wiser heads to counsel
With methods just and fair,
So that thy devoted children
Will find that gem so rare,
That precious, cherished legacy,
That priceless pearl so dear,
A truly just and lasting peace,
When all ills will disappear.
O, then, beloved country,
Thy shores now freed from taints,
Will once more be the cradle
Of scholars and of saints.

Edward Farren

IS FAITH RELIGION OR OBSESSION?
(Sept 11 2001)

The metal cross rose like a phoenix from the ashes
After the tragedy that had buried it that day
It remained as a reminder forever
Of the evil that was done where it stood in the way.

The planes came without warning any thoughts or regrets
Just death to the people they hated, and yet
How can you kill without knowing the person you killed?
Is life so worthless and hatred so weak willed?

Obsession takes over where religion has failed
To justify thoughts of vengeance planted in
                    minds that are veiled.
Why are the sins of the fathers recommitted by the sons?
In the name of peace for their culture, a war's never won.

I'm sure our 'God' whatever faith we believe
Would never sanction murder, destruction and grief
In the name of God the father and the son
In our way we know we worship the same one.

So now it is time for sanity to regain control
Overcome the hatred and whatever faith let our belief extol
Our compassion and charity to our friends and neighbours alike
Whatever race or religion be they black or white.

Let us look to the future of our children in years to come
Ensure that our troubles are not theirs or their years will be none.
There will be no future, all life will be gone
Together with religion, obsession has won!

Sheila M Storr

It Was Just The War

The little old lady was always alone.
She had lost her man in the war.

The ruddy old gent was also alone.
He had buried his wife long before -
After the rubble was cleared.

The little old lady was petite and young long ago.
She danced with the soldier in the palais de danse
And the quick-step mirrored her happy young soul, I know -
I know it because she told my grandmother so - of the chance
She'd once had to be only the soldier's - and his alone.

The ruddy old gent was pink-cheeked and tall long ago.
He'd married his wife as war was declared after a quiet romance
And the rising sun reflected his happy young soul, I know -
I know it because he'd told my grandfather so - of the evil chance
That had blown her to bits while he was at sea - and left him alone.

'Why are you always alone?' they'd said.
'Why didn't you marry again?'
There isn't an answer that can be spoken
When you know that your heart has died - after you've cried!
And you've known bitterness as soon as you've woken
For a long, long time - and sorrow's like rain -
And none can replace the dead.

'It was the war!' they'd said.
'It was just the war!'

S V Batten

SOULS OF SOLDIERS

When stars gaze down from the dark midnight sky
An eerie chill creeps across the Flanders fields.
Young soldiers are marching once again, some only
Lads, not yet grown to men.
Their lonely spirits rise up to walk the muddy
Trenches once more. Some still whistling haunting
Tunes to hide their fear. So brave marching to
Their death, very near.
The one thing for certain, soon they are to die
Those poor young souls to remain forever under
The midnight sky . . . on Flanders fields.

Tracy Mitchell

SUBURBIA

The natives are restless
the spring affecting their brains.
So out they come with their weapons
the shears, the strimmers, the scissors
regardless of who bought the bushes
with pensions saved up for years.
They snip, they cut and they zoom
what price now Britain in bloom?
The birds on the edges tremble
their habitat altered in hours
they leave us for other folks' gardens
natural ones with many wild flowers.
So what has become of our gardens
too neat and too tidy to bear?
No longer a pleasure to sit in
so I will remove to elsewhere.

Joan R Gilmour

Violent Ulster

No human rights, no martyrs fame,
few but family recall their name,
they lie in lonely graves,
alas, murdered for sake of Ireland's impasse.

No time to utter last farewell,
sacrificed for why, only their killer can tell.
Lambs of slaughter without a choice,
thousands have paid this ultimate price.

Grieving loved ones fearfully pray,
Lord end this reign of terror day,
grant that 'the peace process' overcome,
to defeat the bullet and the bomb.

Cease-fire hanging by a thread,
uncertainty for days ahead,
sectarian violence, nightly rage,
have politicians struggling in a maze.

Guns of death may silent be,
and bombs diminished to a few,
but 'hate godfathers' on Ulster prey,
east of the 'Bann River' and
west of Lough Neagh.

Brick and petrol bombs attack,
security forces upon the rack
gangland paramilitary,
'tis Ulster's violent legacy.

A punishment squad, a broken down door,
a defenceless victim upon the floor,
gunshot wounds, broken bones,
kangaroo injustice, the stomach turns.

Bitter widespread anarchy,
is politically inspired insanity,
inbred passions ruling the heart,
leaves little room for love impart.

But despite the warring sections wrong,
love of Ireland burns ever strong,
tolerance is the crying need,
respect for culture, conscience, creed.

Alan Moore

NEW YORK SEPTEMBER 11 2001

I sing no song
For he has gone
He who played the tune.
His sensuous fingers
Sending heart beats soaring,
With fiery passion consumed.
No more songs,
Only a pyre,
A funeral pyre.
For like a meteor descending
He has fallen
With the crumbling Twins.
Titanic towers dissolving
Crushing beloved kin.
I sing no song
For he has gone.
He, who played the tune
Caressing the melody of life along.
He lies silent
In a smouldering tomb.
He has gone,
I sing no song.

M Elizabeth Workman

WAR AND PEACE

Peace is the prelude
Time to orchestrate the symphony score
Nobel peace prize
Form the angels of love
Hell's own angels
Practice to sing
Mozart sweet requiem

Soldiers troop the colours of the realm
Dressed to kill, sing the angels of Hell.
Soldiers sold, sold, body and soul
Rehearse to sing, real rock and roll
Glorious, thunder of guns
Sing Hell's rock and roll
Smell the fire of Hell's own brimstone

Sing, sing real rock and roll
To the crescendo
Of the glorious tunes of war
To the boom of the big guns
Ejaculating death
Lord Kalasnyikov sing the semi quavers of death
Guns and Roses rhyme like
Butter and bread
The Lord of Death, administer the last sacrament

The angels of love sing a duet with
The angels of Hell
To the thunderous roar of the guns
Scream the ejaculating shells of crescendo thunder of death
Silently. The wounded are praying
For the mercy of death
The sacrament of hate is the last sacrament.

T Lawrence

BLASPHEMY

I loved the world so much,
I gave up my only son,
So that no one need be destroyed.

So that children can be free
To go to school in safety.
Not threatened by masked men,
Nor hatred, death, nor violence.

So that people could live in harmony.
Not oppressed by cruel foreign policy,
By the most powerful of affluent nations,
Who built such symbols of domination.

So that Abraham's offspring,
Could live in union.
Let's wage war on the real but barely hidden enemy.
The father of lies, using division as clever strategy.

And those who wage their war,
How dare you name it: Crusade Holy War?
Lies, death and devastation are acts,
Not written in my contract.
Nor abuse, oppression and the cause of pain
Don't use my name in vain!

Some call me God.
Some call me Allah.
Some call me Jehovah.

I am who I am: love, truth, justice, peace, transcendent,
Immanent, infinite, incarnate, compassionate,
Omniscient, immutable, all-enduring,

Yet more than the sum of these . . .

Olga Allen

TIME TO GET IT RIGHT

The terrorists were beside themselves with joy.
At last fate had given them a nuclear weapon.

Fanatically they unleashed its awesome might.
The nuclear powers unwisely responded in kind.

Wearily, the Almighty looked on in great sorrow.
Thoughtfully he contemplated the egg of a dinosaur.

First the terrible lizards, and then cruel man.
For a time both had lorded it over the Earth.

Neither had proved to be an evolutionary success,
Still the desire to kill was far too prevalent.

Life had originated in the bosom of the oceans.
Maybe a complete return to the maritime would work.

Aeons of time to get the cellular structure correct.
Ah well, back to the cosmic drawing board once more.

Richard J Bradshaw

ON THE LONGEST DAY

Fresh powder-blue sky
  dotted with puffball clouds; light
breeze loosening my hair

I follow shadows:
  two little boys are chasing
kites up the hillside

this could not be Kabul
  - or could it? A blackbird's
descent dries my tears

Anna Taylor

MY THOUGHTS OF THE WORLD TODAY

As I lay in my bed and think of the world today,
   to me the wars and massacres are here to stay.
And as I look out of the window and look into the sky,
   there is not a day that goes by, where there is fighting
mass murder and plunder, and to me the world is going under.
   Some politicians of the world are always talking to each other,
with summits here, and summits there, and nothing seems
   to ever come to bear.
This turmoil in the Middle East, oh how I wish this war to cease.
   The solution of this crisis is there, a compromise is there,
but no one on either side, seems to want or care.
   The solution is that, the borders before the seven days
   war be retained, and peace
at last will be regained.
   I wonder when, and how, this solution will come about,
then the populace in joyous raptures will shout.
   But alas, I cannot see this cancer of greed
will always be here to be.

Peter Antonian

FIVE BELLS

The ships that lay on the horizon
Dipped silently into the dawn.
They dotted along dawn's majestic pride
Moving towards the bite,
Give me the sword to do all justice
And I will end the carnage,
For saltness is a man's own colour
And justice man's own pride.

T P Coggins

FRONT LINE

With words they go to battle,
For power and land.
Anticipating an order from a general,
Miles outbound.
Front line is where the real men,
Stand.

Like dutiful dogs they wait in lay,
Marking an indistinguishable,
Border of disguise.
Looking for the foe, thinking of home.
Searching for certainty,
With which they have no doubt.

Politician addresses the nation,
They all stop and listen.
Praising and pleading,
For the men on the front line.
Pawns to play,
Turns, nods at the general's wry smile.

Lead rains on the front line,
Decorating the landscape,
Rubble and the dead.
Politicians come under fire,
Trepidation and opinions,
No bullets.

The wake of the storm is rancid,
In flavour of the psyche.
Politician queries actions taken,
Lives gambled, lives conquered.
All for the cause of a gentleman.

On the front line,
Men lay,
Amongst the wake of the bombs.
Agonised bodies, lifeless.
A breeze scatters the battle-worn sand,
A man's memory falls from his hand.

Byron McAlpine

THE CHANGING FACE OF CONFLICT

Martial arts reflect the chivalry
Which used to mask the bloodiness of war.
But now the heat of battle draws
The furtive missile on its destructive course.
Uniforms and war-paint designed to frighten,
Blend now to hide and distort shape . . .
War is not waged alone by military protagonists,
But cowardly involves civilian lives
Suicides intent to destroy even children,
A gory flag to wave to boost a cause.
God forbid we should revert to trenches,
Or dress men again as scarlet blazing targets -
Turn our backs upon the world's injustices,
And not defend oppressed without a voice;
But let us first ensure the way of freedom,
Peace for all to enjoy all of God's gifts.
Armies set to rebuild not plunder
Bind up the sores of need not wounds of war.
Dogs of war unleashed are hard to muzzle,
Scythes of hate lay a land to waste,
Little flares of anger grow to conflagration,
Generations bred to perpetuate a hate.
The world must find strength to curb the destrier
Not ride helm down into the global fray.

Di Bagshawe

HONOUR YOUR MOTHER

'Honour your mother,'
This was the Lord's commandment,
To Jane, one daughter
'Let go of all resentment.
Cantankerous she has been,
Causing scene after scene,
Still, she remains your loving mother.
You left your mother,
When marriage vows once making,
Life with your lover
From that time undertaking
Your mother is in need,
You must to her proceed
And be her ever loving daughter.'
So, Jane, that daughter,
With John, her well beloved,
Went to her mother,
Real change they both discovered
Soon was Mum's health restored,
Of love much reassured,
Then there were tears and also laughter.
Their heavenly Father
Looked down on His creation,
With utmost pleasure,
Saw reconciliation.
Jane had him well obeyed,
So that true peace was made
'Twixt partner, daughter and her mother.

D J Price

BANG!

Bang!
The golden sun in torment cries
As dust clouds fall and black palls rise
To spoil an otherwise perfect sky.
Bang! . . . The briefest silence, unforgiving,
Then cries and frantic screams from the living,
As paused time races back into line.
Bang! . . . Numbed, confused, emotions run rife.
Relief; shared grief; fragile life
That all hangs in the balance of fate.
Bang! . . . A scene freely splattered in red,
Daubed on the injured, bystanders . . . the dead,
And the tangle of limbs in the debris.
Bang! . . . An act that deepens the divide
Where war is groom and death the bride,
And all their offspring are doomed to know pain . . .
Bang! . . . Blow all tomorrows away
As hatred stalks the streets today
Tainting all that it touches.
Bang! . . . Terror grips the streets once more,
Where the chill of fear, of death, and more,
Lies heavy on battle-weary hearts.
Bang! . . . Death sounds its mournful horn
Claiming all hope, born and unborn,
And closes the door on the future.
Bang! . . . And who knows the reason why
The living bomb is prepared to die,
And why life itself is so cheap?
Bang! . . .

Bryan Davies

WAR

How can a life be fulfilled
When death looms near on grimace fields,
When skies light up with murderous tones,
Hideous flesh lay staring and cold;
Crouch amongst the stench and filth
Shake and tremble with fear or quilt,
Past lives that had a joyous tale,
All for human lust for gain.

Generals bleat 'Kill! Kill! Kill or die!'
More souls are lost, they know not why;
I'm forced to lay ashen the gift of this land,
Rip out its heart and hold it high,
With black scorching searing hate
Wrench the sinews and bones of states;
Then stand proud like rods of steel,
For the feat it took, and the cost to heal.

All alone I'm allowed to cry,
To leave behind the insane crime,
Forget about the blood and dammed,
Fulfil a life without stained hands;
But still the grief and anguish prevail,
Those haunting eyes of those I slayed,
The horror! Grotesquely dancing in dreams,
Unholy violence; dipped, in screams.

Shane Stephens

No Savoir

With slippery tongue,
You stab enough to scar.
A falling star.
You have no savoir.

Sitting with headphones, whispering my demise,
You are a studio bully! You victimise.
Laying it in the tracks of every spinning disc,
I hear you full of revenge, as you take such risk.
But you are a coward of the first degree,
Dubbing it all over, harassing so secretly.
Dishonouring our friendship, why should that be?
With such criticism, talking violently.

You try to torment,
Just never relent.
I will not lament.
You are fraudulent!
Is this punishment?
Such embitterment,
For this predicament.
You need enlightenment.

You will never win this spar.
I am stronger and braver than you are.
You are a studio bully!
With no savoir.

Tali Rose

REPENT

Repent, repent, put down your weapons,
lay aside your hatred, repent,
forget your petty squabbles and your violent ways,
cease to maim hurt, kill and hate,
forgive thine enemies as thy forgives thyself of sins and mistakes,
see thine enemy as thyself, put down your arms and tools of destruction,
show thine enemy no malice, throw flowers, not hand grenades,
shake not your spears and swords in anger,
but shake one another's hand in gesture of peace and goodwill,
make bonds not bombs,
forgive others their faults for their faults are yours.
See thine enemy as thy brother and sisters,
do not all siblings fight when young,
but one day not grow up and feel strong for each other?
Is it not wiser to make friends not enemies
and to have compassion not hatred?
Is vengeance the answer? If you forget thou shalt not kill,
you are killing someone's father, sister, mother, daughter,
sons or brother, you are killing yourself,
when you kill another, stop, listen, look, think,
do not kill your own brother.
Live in peace and harmony, strive to be happy,
share your happiness and goodwill with others,
give up bad vibes and negative thoughts,
life is bigger than any one man, situation or cause,
and no cause is worth killing for, all life is precious,
not to be taken on the whim of a capricious soldier
or misguided person allegedly a terrorist.
Once more repent, repent, give up your anger, fear and loathing,
put down your weapon and live in peace,
give peace a chance, violence only engenders more violence
and is not an answer, give up your inner turmoil,
relax, chill out, learn to meditate,
and amidst the noise, rush and confusion,
remember what peace there is in silence,

take a moment to stop and ponder,
and see what beauty and good there is in the world,
let your mantra be 'Bitza eta undi bitzen', or in other words
'Live and let live', life is too short to hold grudges
or fight about something that happened in the past,
live for today for it does not last, life is for living, not for killing.
Peace be with you brother and sister.
Om beni-baubmay um, om benishiva,
amor bensit omnia et omnia est amor. Pax cum botis et ahimsa, Bil.

Bill Williams

THE SKIRMISH

Battle lines are drawn
Eyes glitter and gleam
Neither side can be seen
From where I'm sitting
On the lawn

A deep rumble from here
A long hiss from there
A spitting yelling noise
Disturbs the quiet air

My peace is shattered
Fur flying ginger
And tabby white
I'm in the middle of a fight

To the kitchen I retreat
And two saucers fill with meat
Peace is declared
All is still while my two cats
Eat their fill on the mats

Joy M Bufton

PEACE, PEACE, BUT THERE IS NO PEACE

There is a small piece of land in the Middle East.
It has seen war of over 50 years.
Two peoples claim it and refuse to share it.
Yet they are related to each other.
Both are Semites and claim Abraham as their father.
Both Hebrew and Arabic are sister languages.
So why is there far more hatred than love?
The very soil is drenched with the blood of the innocent.
Men, women, children, babies -
All have been bloody victims.
Is there a way for the two related people to come together in harmony?
Only by compromise and mutual respect can things change
                                           for the better.
Both pray to the same God, though the name be Adonai or Allah.
Let them remind each other that they are children of the same One God.
Pursue peace for the sake of your children and their children.
Then all will enjoy God's most precious gift of Shalom-Saalam.

Douglas Charing

OMAGH STACCATO

The searing brightness heralds
Deep growls of devastation
Timeless seconds of disbelief
Then frenzied chaos, smash and crush.

Blinding dust, cloying, clogging
Silence sits in anticipation
Now as if by given signal
A howl of torment rips the air.

Like some demented orchestra
These damaged instruments
Shriek and wail, beat and drum
Others will never play the tune.

What composer scored this anthem
With harsh discordant melody
Can he transpose this mad recital
Create symphonic harmony.

Marylee Rounce

1914-1918

It was memory souring the song in his head
and bitterness that left an emptiness in his life,

but when the memory was taking shape
he was that simmering barrel of faith and hope;
one was blind, the other cautious.

A long bony finger pointed the way.
It led him smiling, uncomplaining
closer to the quivering edge.

The sun was in his eyes
and the rousing song,
the rhythmic footfall
left him unaware that

the flesh of the finger
was pale from the sight of death
and the nail brown with the
scrapings of blood stained mud.

Godfrey Dodds

THE ARMOUR OF GOD

We fight a battle every day,
As sin rules in every heart.
But praise our God, He gives the weapons,
And the armour that we need.

A powerful enemy we have to overcome,
The devil seems to have full sway.
He seems to take control of many things,
But praise God, one day, he'll have had his day.

Meanwhile, we must arm ourselves really well.
Fill ourselves with His Holy Spirit,
Gird our loins with Jesus the truth.
Put the breastplate of righteousness upon our breast.
Prepare our feet with the gospel of peace.
Take hold with our hands the shield of faith.
Place upon our head the helmet of salvation,
And take in the other hand, ready to use,
The sword of the spirit, the precious word of God.
And let our whole body be clothed with the garment of prayer.
Always being watchful and alert to our enemy's tactics.
For the wiles of the devil are very devious,
Creeping into our lives so unexpectedly.

Praise God, we do not fight the battle alone,
He Himself is there to strengthen and sustain us,
To guide us and direct us, as we lend a conscious ear,
Listen well, and be ready to obey, then and then only,
Shall we be able always, to win the day.
The battle will not be lost, it will be ours,
In the name of the Father, Son and Holy Ghost.

R Baker

THE AFTERMATH

I stood transfixed, for at my feet
A hand - a baby's hand I saw.
It lay there gently in the dust.
Little fingers lightly curled.
Severed wrist - now fringed with 'rust'.
A tiny alabaster hand -
Held softly now within mine own.
So light, so frail and scarcely cold -
It lay there, still and so alone.
No tight clenched trauma did it show.
Nor wide stretched fingers, as in fear,
But reaching out and sweetly curled
As if it had a gift to share.

Was the babe, a while ago
Smiling at his mother's face -
Hand held out - to take or give
In another time - another place?
I stood there lonely, deep in thought.
Would this hand, when fully grown
Have given help to weak and old
Reached out to babies of its own?

I felt the coolness on my palm
'Let me go' - it seemed to say.
'I'll stay in sexless innocence -
My time is gone - I'm far away!'
Since then a thousand baby hands
Are being stilled by war and strife.
When will we learn - when will it be
That *all* find peace and joy and *life*?

Margaret A P Quinn

THE SOLDIER'S LAST WORDS
(The Great War 1914-18)

As the enemy rushed our trench; we were truly all but done.
'You'd better make room in Heaven Lord, 'cause in a moment
here I come.'
Those were the words I bellowed, there in panic down on my knees.
Screaming to God the Almighty to make room in Heaven please.

I think I've tolerated enough Lord, so give me one last chance.
Extract me from this land Lord, this battlefield in France.
I've suffered many indignities Lord, from bullet and from shell.
So St Peter open them gates wide, 'cause I'm ready to leave this Hell.

As whistling shrapnel pierced my chest, a smile came to my face,
For I knew that I was going now to a far more happy place.
As I floated in tranquillity, drawn by a light high in the sky,
A vision of my mother I saw, and a tear was in her eye.

'Don't shed a tear for me Mother' I roared and then I wailed.
To reach my mother's ears though, I'm afraid my message failed.
So readers of this sonnet, please ease my mother's dolour,
Tell her I love her dearly, much more than I did before.

Garry Knowles

AGAIN AND AGAIN

It's happening again and again
The pain, the bloodshed and sorrow.
When this battle for justice is done
It will happen elsewhere tomorrow.

Words we thought we would never hear again
Pogram, Holocaust and slaughter.
Are featured on the evening news
A mother, a husband, a daughter.

Whole families, communities wiped out again
Because their god has a different name.
When will mankind realise,
No matter what we choose to believe
We are all genetically the same?

The world is shedding tears again
We try to stop their cries
Yet for every thousand lives we save
Another thousand dies.

Derek Blackburn

DARKNESS OF OUR AGE

So bland are the footsteps of man's ego - some
awareness awakens his thoughts as not before

Deep, dark ravines and mystic chasms now replace the
one time clarity of mind - no joyous message or gay
acclaim to behold

Many tomorrows have come and gone - some
bringing joy through birds of song - others more forlorn

Grey mists creeping also, unfolding with alarm and
man in desperation looking for calm

No tragedy like avalanche of whiteness to emerge, no
earthen tremor to convulse or volcano to erupt

The vastness of time as we know - or even since time
began, its magnitude so great

Could it be from man's earthly slumber arrives the
fateful tomorrow - that holocaust void of any meaning.

Lyndon Thomas

HOW DO WE TELL THE CHILDREN?

How do we tell the children
Of the people that were there?
How do we explain to them,
Of the terror, from the air?
How can we console the loved ones left
In their hours of despair?
How can our children understand,
Why we cry, though we're not there?

How do we tell the children
Of the concrete, glass and steel?
How can we explain to them,
That the buildings there, were real?
How do we tell the rescue teams
Don't worry, you'll be fine,
When they all know the enemy now,
Is the struggle against time?

How do we tell the children
Why terrorist yearn to die?
How can they ever understand
How can they ever try?
Or will they ever comprehend,
The anguish and despair,
That where historic buildings stood
Death himself, is waiting there?

How can we tell the children
It's they that hold the keys?
The keys to worldly love
And their hearts must nurture peace
To shape our future world,
And not to create hate.
It's they, the children hold the keys
To our Earth's future fate.

Leslie F Higgins

NO ONE REMEMBERS THE HEROES

Take a look at your face in the mirror
Count the lines that have grown as you've aged.
Drink a toast from your half glass of bitter
To the memory of Robert Paul Grace.
Your best friend was killed in a battle
On the 18th of June '43
'Though he stopped the full shot with your name on
You can't help but still feel Rob is free.

But you're proud of your meagre possessions.
Your small house would be fit for a king.
Life is worth more than material things.
You've been robbed of your medals and rings.
They can't steal away all your memories.
'Though these days they're much harder to find.
And you've lain awake crying the whole night
With nightmares that still trouble your mind.

Now you've saved enough money to go back
Find you best friend's name carved on a wall
Crack open a small bottle of bitter.
Drink a toast to the best of them all.
Remember the times you both cherished
All the nights you had out on the town.
The smile on Rob's face, he told you the name
Of the girl who'd wear his wedding gown.

For no one remembers the heroes
From a war that was fought far from home.
Each day becomes more of a struggle
Payment for the bravery you showed.

Damien Aked

ISRAEL

I saw this bright crimson-red poppy
At the side of a tank
An awesome combination of colour
That would befit any artist's palette,
In the rubble of the roadside the poppy,
On the road itself the domineering tank
Raining death and terror
To any who dare.
In the distance
A young child falls to her knees
She is crying as she pleads,
And as the crimson-red stain
Bursts through her dress,
An explosion erupts in the tank
To leave a hell for those within.
And as I climbed to my feet
Deaf and alone,
I saw this bright crimson-red poppy
Beside the roadside
All alone.

Phillip A Taylor

BABY BLUES

A life as dear as a new born child,
A mother in pain giving birth, she cries, she whimpers.
The corridor silent, still.
The doctors in uniform pass by, step by step,
The sound it echoes.

The children cry in a broken down ward in Africa.
No mother in pain, no doctors, just walls plain.

Kathryn Bocking

QUALQUILIA
(West Bank town - circa 85)

Guns aimed on Tel Aviv in 68
backwater, breeze block, coffee shop
open sewers, extended families, humility

Guns aimed at Tel Aviv in 68
kids scavenging through the kibbutz waste, timeless olive groves,
vegetable plots, dirt roads, dirty faces, humanity

Guns aimed at Tel Aviv in 68
dark cool nights, humus eaten out of newspaper
the family home, platters of everything for our English guests

A football match, table tennis in the cafe
trips to Nablus and Jerusalem - curfew, West Bank passes checked
pity Jamaal was carrying a knife

Guns aimed,
land day,
town cordoned off

Charles Webster

THE PEACE ROSE

The Rose of Peace is gentle,
Its golden, glowing heart,
Tinged with the pink of sunrise.
War, and its hideous weapons,
Casts a dark shadow
Of death and destruction.
But the Peace Rose will bloom
With an even greater beauty,
To transform a disillusioned world.

U Johnson

WAR AND PEACE

After the dissipations of St Petersburg,
The struggle to defend Sebastopol,
The war in the Crimea and the Caucasus,
After titanic labours at his desk, and all

The business of Sophia Andreyevna and the serfs,
After the years of wrestling with belief
And the abandonment of all his earthy goods,
He turned towards the land to find relief.

The last time he was happy was at Kochety,
A visit to the Sukhotins. Though snow
Was imminent, he set off walking, in the dusk, alone.
They found him on a fallen tree, singing about a crow

That, solitary, flew away into the dark,
Impenetrable wood from which return's impossible.
He wanted quietness, sought simplicity.
He found them, but the quest was terrible.

Quitting the house in which he had been born,
He knelt and kissed the grass: first of his stations of the cross,
Yasnaya Polyana, where, in spring, the scent of lilac
Filled the air. Ancient as Lear, he felt its loss

A rapier thrust. Past turnip fields, he took the rutted track
Towards Kozelsk, milkweed and mullein poking through
The wintry crust. At last, at Astapovo, he found peace.
The wind moaned softly in Zasyeka Wood, sifting the snow.

Norman Bissett

SIGH TODAY AS WOMAN BECOMES VEG
DAILY CHRONICLE

Lives destroyed every day -
'Man Sacked', 'Sex Scandal', headlines say.
Who am I then to cry my woe
When I have friends to whom I can go
To discuss my minor pains?

What can she do who is raped?
Or he that is maimed?
Only when my arms too are torn from their sockets
Will I even begin to know
The intensity of Irish misery and woe.

Blood may be thick, but it runs so fine . . .
Used as the ink of the morning headline.
'Leg Blown Off', 'Death Toll 25',
Can any of this murder be justified?

She once loved me, till she lost her mind
Gone because she committed the offence of crossing the line . . .
Leg off at knee, arms gone complete,
Her mind hides, frozen in some dark retreat.
Too afraid to live, life gone in a sigh
Drained of so much we cannot even cry.

Sectarian violence . . . it's religiously just
Tell that to the innocents whose lives have been crushed.

Robert Harrison

LOVE AND PEACE

Let hate, my friends not burn up our souls
And make our hearts as hard as brick and stone.
Spite, revenge and hate are firebrands of Satan's filthy spawn.
While love is a shining star that comes from God's right hand.
Let not our eyes ever close in sleep serene
Until we have made our peace with fancied foes.
Yesterday's wrongs are dead and gone
Tomorrow brings a brighter day.
Harsh words and threats of dire revenge
Can only harm ourselves and bring furrows to our brow.
Our hearts were made to swell with love
Our minds to harbour only kindly thoughts.
Love and peace go hand in hand along a sunny path.
And every soul our maker put on Earth
Has divine purpose just like us.

Brigid O'Donnell

A GAME OF HEARTS

Circle above looking down from the sky;
You're lost in thoughts while the sun's standing high.
She will not hear you, 'cause silent's your cry.
You stand unshielded, your heart's lying bare,
But my heart in full armour does not care;
I tilt with passion, not noble or fair.
You come to me in your weakest hour,
Strong and upright I stand like a tower;
Love's but a game, pitting power 'gainst power,
The firing of guns, the crossing of blades,
Light the candles before the daylight fades;
Blinded by hearts you draw the queen of spades.
The daylight's gone, fake gems are glowing bright;
You try to hide from them in the abyss of night.

Lucy E Lutzke

HEAR... O ISRAEL

Fresh green leaves, cover each mountain and hillside . . .
A sight not seen for almost 200 years in this land of the miraculous . . .
Another miracle appears . . . each tiny blade of grass, each plant, each flower . . . stretches heavenward, responsively, in vanguard of each shower . . .
The raindrops being new scents . . . new aromas . . . and, senses are aroused . . . such as . . . never have been felt . . . at home.
And . . . all is not at peace . . . all is not quiet . . .
For . . . mixed amongst the perfumes of nature . . . there are others . . .
Cordite . . . gun-oil . . .
As . . . Jew, Arab, and Christian strive to . . . live, work, and die . . . side by side . . .
Hear, O Israel . . . and mark well with discerning 'eye'!

Lew Park

THE TERRORIST

Has he won do you think
Has he answered his call?
Condemned by most
Hounded by all,
Has he at last
Found evil cannot win
Cannot overcome?
May this spirit of ours
Keep us together,
May the wish for peace
Keep us together.
We can only pray
For East and West
To become *us*.

Mary Cole

I AM YOU WE ARE THEY

I am the gun
           so fire me
I am the man
           so hire me
Together we will destroy you

You are to blame
           so face it
You chose the field
           so grace it
With every rotting bone

We are the expendables
           so spend us
We are the fodder
           so blend us
In the war machine

They lie in silky down
           so wake them
They invest in blood and tears
           so make them
Spill their own

John Marshall

HOPE

Will the apparitions of Holy persons
Bring the peace so desired by many,
And change the evils of war and killings
To peaceful coexistence?

Will the love power of The Holy Spirit
Penetrate the evil minds of persons,
Trained to destroy God's creations,
To understand and love again?

Will their New Writings become The Way for all
As one new re-creation for life in peace,
And thus save future lives and lands?
I hope The Holy Spirit win.

M Andrews

JUST A THOUGHT

If there was no war
Would there be peace?
Would we all be friends
Or acquaintances at least?

Have you seen the film
Schlinder's List?
It's so cruel it really
Does take the P***

I wonder if war
Could ever stop
Would all the arguments
Just be dropped?

Is peace all it's
Cracked up to be?
Do you reckon there'll be
A world War III?

If there was there'd be
No chance for peace,
We'd never be friends
Or acquaintances at least.

Deborah Foley

NO PEACE ON EARTH

I often wonder why it is that man must always fight,
It seems so senseless - so insane!
It simply isn't right.
Though other species often feud
Over habitats, and food,
They must do this to stay alive -
No other way will they survive.
But man is far above all that -
Or so he claims, I've heard:
The human is superior
To animal, fish or bird,
With a better brain, he is more humane,
So kind, and loving too: if that is true
Then why do beings of that sort
Behave as devils do?
Many preach 'the word of God' -
The One they claim to love -
Yet still they kill, ignoring all
Instructions 'from above'.
As we all know, God's basic law
Is 'Thou shalt not kill',
So why does man behave like this,
Defying his God's will?
'Love thy neighbour as thyself'
Is another rule unheeded;
All that many seem to do
Is to indulge their hatred.
The future now looks very bleak
For people on this planet;
Sadly, my conclusion is 'We've had it!'

F Hodgkinson

BETHLEHEM 2002

Suppose He had been born today
in an occupied country.
Joseph would have telephoned for an ambulance
because it was her first
and they had nowhere to go.
The walls of the inn had been smashed by tanks
so they were hiding in the cellar.

The ambulance was shot at anyway,
two paramedics died. No one came.
He was born, placed in an old basin.
There was no water:
a bomb had split the main.
He was wrapped in a dirty towel
still stiff with the innkeeper's blood.

Suppose the shepherds had tried to visit?
They wouldn't have got through the cordon.
Shot before they got close
in case their warm clothes were just a disguise
and they were intending to blow up the command post.
And the lamb would have been highly suspect.

The wise men from the east
would never have made it past Jerusalem.
Their camel train torn apart
in search for illegal weapons.
Their gifts blown up
just in case they were booby-trapped.

And both sides would report
that missiles were fired from helicopter gun-ships
to counter a potential aerial assault.
The angels never stood a chance.

Alix Brown

ANOTHER HAND

With callous force the hand of fear extends itself,
Clenched for retribution, reaching out to catch and crush:
Dark the shadow over those displaced and disenfranchised,
Death an almost daily visitor to where they dwell in deep resentment.

She was just another Arab face along the street
Until the garments of her vengeance ripped the daily round apart,
And every Jew she thus destroyed became a prize;
Hatred's trophies, lives reduced to bald statistics in the press.

Men of so-called power and influence line up to plead:
Motions tabled, motions passed, condemnation by the ream.
But fear and hatred lie in wait with appetites renewed
As Allah and Jehovah cut the cards to play another hand.

Bob White

LOST PROPERTY

My heart burst near to Korea,
as my toes curled to Heaven in Afghanistan,
whilst my prowess was lost in Nigeria
as my legs marched for the freedom of Spain.

My eyes were blinded near Cambodia,
as my reason failed in the Sudan,
whilst my fears sought courage in Bosnia,
as my nerves shattered close to Iran.

If all war should end
and they put me together again,
they'd find that some pieces are missing
in a world that has gone insane.

Jules A Riley

TERRORIST

The two of us
In deadly trim
Face each other
Across the ring
One is crescent
One is cross
One is black
One is white
It does not matter
Who you fight
One is orange
One is green
We are the vilest
You have ever seen
We will not live
We will not die
Our cause is just
You hear us cry
Our cities crumble
Our children scream
No sight more sad
Will ever be seen
The funeral pyre
Is always hot
The hearse is always
At the trot
But the two of us
In deadly trim
Still face each other
Across that ring.

J Stenning

A Schoolchild At War

I'm not quite sure how it began,
Or how it came to an end . . .

A dash of early morning sunrise gold,
And a stroke of calm and collected blue.
A sense of silent noise
And shaking hands.

'Time's up' called out the supervisor of our group,
'Put everything down.'

The supervisor surveyed our colours and styles.
The weapons used to create our masterpieces.
Like a lion marking its prey,
Or an eager mother watching over her child.

Sometimes   he   was   slow   looking   around,
Taking   in   every   detail

Often he was quick.

Everyone looked around for a 'good luck' smile from a friend
Or comrade over the uneven floor,
And noticed a sly glance from a bully or enemy across the
                                          marsh-coloured tiles.

Now, the sunrise gold is a muddy and boggy brown,
And the calm and collected blue is a furrowed brow red.
The silent noise is now the bang, boom, and scream of bombs
And the shaking hands are covered in sweat and guilt-ridden blood.

Nothing's the same now,
Not that you can remember,
You never can when you're at war . . .

The only state of mind you have is hatred and death.
Bullets shoot past and towards you,
Your heart has
          rapid   and
                uneven
beats.

Like when the supervisor marked my piece . . .

. . . I think I passed.

. . . I'm not so sure here . . .

. . . When I'm a schoolchild at war.

Thomas Harrison (15)

WAR

Flashing steel in the sun
Hands clenched tightly
On sword and gun
Bugles sound
The charge is on
As man and horse start their run
Cannons fire from the back
Fill the air with mighty crack
Bodies fall upon the ground
Never to hear another sound
All around destruction near
As man and beast show their fear
Bugler sounds the last all clear
The stench of death will never clear
The war is over but never won
As long as man, kills a mother's son.

John Edney

KABUL WOMEN

What have we done
That you should treat us
Thus?

Peanut butter, daisy cutter
We deserve only
These?

Children know little but war;
Who will work to alter
That?

Death will surely come;
Can we not live a little
First?

Must you have your oil
At the cost to us,
Of all?

Julie Longman

UNTITLED

Fighting a war
Personal genocide
Slightest movement, word or gesture
War paint on
Each advance, a retrogression
Another wound, a victory
Constant
Until too weak to fight anymore
The cause gone
The battle won
By the loser.

Catherine Fleming

THE POOR BUGGER

Taken from his career, his family and his friends
Off to a war that might well bring his end,
That's what's in store when war is about,
When he's needed to carry out policies of Shout and Clout,
The poor bugger.

He is chosen to fight by *'them'* at the top,
His views and wishes are not considered a lot,
It's always the same with their war games,
But he's needed as before, again and again,
The poor bugger.

It's do that, on the double, and that and again that,
And there's no chance of even a nice friendly chat,
Then it's overseas to fight a foe he doesn't know,
But it's someone just like *him* that he'd like to know,
The poor bugger.

He wants to go home after the fight,
And hopes he'll survive and then hopes that he might,
He wants to see his family and friends soon again, then,
But he knows he'll be lucky if he survives to the end.
The poor bugger.

Why can't *'them'*, who are in charge of such wonderful things,
Like *peace* and *security* between nations, bring
Something we want in the future and thus,
Stop this nonsense of always calling on *us,*
The poor bugger.

Leslie Loader

It's Gonna Explode

Once again, the lion opens its mouth and I
Put my head inside its maw, once again, the
Barrel rests against my temple - click-click-click,
Damn this lottery! I pull the pin on a
Grenade, throw it down, then pick it up, it's
Gonna explode, but I don't scare - she says
It's OK, she said it won't happen - it did!
So I stick my fingers in the light socket,
Stab my fingers into the flame to get burned,
Time and time again, always thinking, that,
This time, next time - it won't hurt no more
And I won't get burned - yet I always do
And she says it's my fault, once she said 'Would
You like salt with your wounds?' I said no
But got some anyway.
See, I know it's kind of bad for me, but I
Can't react, for my heart is taken and
My love is blind, let my sacrifice be to
Your liking, if my suffering be your food then
Your hunger is dull to the sharpness of my pain.

Charles Darkly

The Road To Peace With Afghanistan In Mind

The road to peace is a long, long road
With guns firing and bombs falling.
Never resting by day nor night
And death, only calling.
Little children weeping sadly
For fathers never seen again.
Broken homes and broken lives,
Who then is to blame?

Dear Lord of all the universe,
Will the day never come
When Afghanistan will be free
From the loud cry of the deafening drum?
Look on this war-torn country Lord,
Make all hatred cease,
Raise up once more all broken hopes
And give the people peace.

Mary Ferguson

PEACE NOT WAR!

In this world of beauty, of peace and its surrounds
war and hatred still abound . . .
The fellowship of man is held within my hands
as I travel troubled lands . . .
No guns, no grenades held within my grasp
just a cobbler's last . . .
In peace, as nature had intended that I travel
no armoury, no gavel . . .
No dogs of war snapping at my heels
only the love my heart feels . . .
Nature's beauty denuded by cannon fire
a lack of love as they aspire . . .
To destroy man's faith, not only of himself
but of nature and her wealth . . .
For in this world, where beauty can still be found
the toll of death still sounds . . .
For in this Garden of Eden, buried inches deep,
mines still make wives and mothers weep . . .
Is the wastebasket of life, emptied only when we die,
do you hear the orphans cry . . .
When will the dogs of war be shackled in their cage?
I fear my friend, not now, or in this age.

Nicholas Maughan

THE DUEL
A tribute

Beyond our comprehension.
Destruction born of hate.
Twin towers yielded helplessly . . .
 their terrifying fate.
The world observed in horror.
Lives expunged by murder,
that changed the course of history
and altered life forever.
Vengeance was the first response.
The cry for war was dominant.
An 'eye for an eye' . . . the battle cry.
Death to Bin Laden imminent.
As the haunting scene unfurled
'minds' paused to think again.
Afghans were starving . . . dying
in their bleak austere terrain.
Poverty claimed a million lives
as people fed on grass.
No hope. No homes. No sustenance.
Impenetrable impasse.
Countries forged a common bond
to rid the world of terror.
Others chanted; 'Holy War,
Jihad to America.'
As New York grieves and
mourns the dead,
the world reflects upon the cause;
to question 'why' such hatred burns
defying consequence and laws?
A dual response has now evolved
to terminate the terror
and feed the starving multitudes
'caught up' in abject horror.

Keeping faith with ~~~
They blew the town apart;
Screams, as bodies split asunder,
The ground a butcher's mart.

This was Omagh's carnival
On an August afternoon,
Smiling faces young and older
Obliterated soon, too soon.

Help and despair walked hand in hand
As frantically they searched,
Unearthing golden innocents
That humanity besmirched.

Tainted the hands of terrorists,
For mindlessly they wreaked
Dire havoc on that fateful day,
Bleak souls with evil streaked.

Sleep easy in your beds tonight,
You will wake tomorrow.
Not so your victims killed today,
Gone forever, bequeathing sorrow.

Angela Walder

INSANITY

How often have we heard the old excuse, 'But he's insane.
He must be stopped'? It was said of Hitler and Hussein.
Our glorious forces, eyes afire with jingoistic zeal
Are trained only as killing machines, not to think or feel.
To be born the wrong side of a man-made borderline
Deserved the penalty of death by bullet, bomb or mine.
One word from those in power, and any race or creed
Can now be hated enemies, foul in thought and deed.
They may be our allies next time, perhaps were in battles past.
But the present's all that matters, and for that our armies vast
Will trample them, slaughter them, blow them to kingdom come,
No reason needed other than the country they come from.
An insane leader's madness is dangerous when it's spread,
But no more than the brainwashing of hatred, fear and dread.
How many people stop to think of both sides of the story?
To compensate for death and loss, we've corpses draped in glory.
Rousing marches drowned out by the sobs of anguished mourning.
While the dead can hear no music, see no day of victory dawning.
What use is all the pride and pomp, whose benefit is it for?
For those who hide in safety behind a lead-lined Whitehall door.
Cheap trade routes, oil prices, it's the economy that rules.
For this we are disposable, fed sophist's lies like fools.
They persuade us and convince us that right is on our side,
Because for money-makers the human cost is justified.
And they said Hitler was mad!

Stephanie Harness

BLITZED

London, Dresden, Coventry
Will never fade from memory
Of those who do recall the nights'
And mornings' devastating sights.

So please forgive us who deplore
Carpet and cluster bombs galore
Raining down, ever intense,
To kill one crook! Not innocence?

Sigrid Armitage

WAR AND PEACE

The opposing forces of war and peace
alternate together in a tumult
of power which will never cease.

War embodies everything that is black
while peace suggests all that is white.
Like the colours of a newspaper they exist together
as the black print relies on the white pages
to inform its readers of the latest developments.

As the pages blacken with the news of war
we are confronted with scenes of death,
burnt out buildings and wreckages of cars.
There is the darkness of downcast sorrow
as mourners in black weep for innocent lives.

The days go forth, exhausted by war,
there is a temporary cease-fire.
The pages now print news of peace.
White for a time predominates with scenes
of lilies and marble paying tribute to the dead.
There is a calmness and serenity as
tormented minds are subdued with suffering
but after a while the pages turn, returning to black.
The wounds heal, but the scars remain.

Sharon Ferguson

BORDERLINE

You have come back to me
crying, from the hills,
down through crumbling walls
and stumbling stones.

I waited at the border
repeating your name,
willing you to live,
praying to Allah.

So now, what can I do
but stroke your hair,
matted with sweat and semen.
wash you and wash you
in the stream, cold water
easing the pain.

I crush Arnica flowers
to lay on your bruises,
hold you close,
rock you and rock you
'til the crying ceases.

Outwardly calm,
inwardly fraught.
Fearful am I
for your future
and the life within.

Linda P Brookes

WHAT IS PEACE?

What is peace?
An absence of war?
I think not -
The presence of justice?
Perhaps
Justice for all perhaps?
Very difficult.

A quiet mind?
If only . . .
Practising stillness?
Possibly.

Acceptance of what
Cannot be changed?
Surely this means
Striving for what can?

Justice for the poor
Enabling self-sufficiency
And self-respect.

Fair dealings
In trade
In what we buy . . .
From whom we buy . . .

Peace is a daily need
A daily prayer
Peace within
The road to God.

Caroline Pybus

RED IN CONTRAST

A sea of glorious red in jubilation at World Cup fever.
A burst of evil red as terror-focused minds
Blast thousands to their death.

Pools of wasted red when crazed fanatics
Blow themselves and other lives apart
To justify land greed and doubtful hope
Of post-suicidal glory.

But red, too, is the colour of sunrise,
Proclaiming new starts, fresh hopes.
A chance to forgive and begin again.

Sunset red spreads across the changing sky
Bringing a challenge to revisit the day
And ask its purpose for peace, near and far.

Contrasts of lives. Contrasts of motives.
Joy alongside joyless destruction.
Man's capacity for spreading good or brooding evil.

The red of joy, beauty and fruitful challenge
Must overcome the red of sorrow, grief and greed,
And the real meaning of religious faith, at last,
Proclaimed and lived in every land.

Then man can live in peace, so long striven for
In church and state, and the first colour
Of the rainbow of hope, becomes the colour
Of new beginnings, for neighbour, country,
And every individual heart.

Margaret Heavenor

OSAMA BIN LADEN

Osama bin Laden, by sin so laden
Yet, a man of wealth and means
He came from Saudi Arabia it seems
Worth all of 300 million pounds I recall
So how can he watch the Afghanistans fall?
Poor as they are, could he not provide
More, not less, security for them, prove to be on their side?
Instead of teaching young Arabs to war
Instead of training suicidal maniacs, what is more
Could he not teach them to till the field
And food instead grow, golden grain then to yield?
With millions of pounds what could he do?
At least make a start, or would that seem too good to be true?
Poorer still they will be and how, have they not
Really suffered enough somehow?
And over how many years? 20 odd years or more it is now
Yet one man, see but one man alone, came here to Earth
To do just what? Seek first a throne?
No! Die to atone and for man's sin and he did suffer too
Deserted by friends, even family, yes! And the Jew his own to be true.
They had him nailed to a tree, Jesus Christ for all to see
Yet did he complain? Indeed he did not, believe you me,
Though he suffered in agony.
He had no 300 million pounds either, we see
For he died too from sin, set all mankind free
And also, from no doubt, the Afghanistans' sheer loss and poverty
Of both body and soul
Osama bin Laden, you are in the wrong, you must see as a whole.

Margaret Lightbody

Why?

Why in this world of trouble and strife
The aim is to battle and disfigure all life?
A heart which desires an abundance of love
Is gifted and merciful and graced from above.
Such inner spheres of goodness and faith
Swell from the depths of the soul's secret place.
Enkindled with peace, deep down in our will
Is the spirit of love where no evil can dwell.
To be patient and kind, to share all we possess
To see only one colour in this world of unrest.
Even more to speak easy with nations at war
And show them we love them that little bit more.
We're in this together from birth to the grave
Let's pass on the peace which Christ freely gave.

Hilary Barton

Shalom - Salem

Israel, struggle, political debate
Pro-Palestinian, war, violence, hate,
Flags, triumphantly flown on each divide,
Ammunition, human, bodies supplied.
Delegation, meetings, proposals presented,
Political, foreign, input resented,
A mother, a child, a father slaughtered,
A mother, a child, a father martyred.
Jerusalem, Jerusalem the city of peace,
Will compromise conquer, and hatred cease?
When the children can sing freely,
Israel, our homeland, this is where we belong,
And the ravages of war are buried and gone.

Linda Levy

WAR AND PEACE

I am alone
The last man standing
On the lonely battlefield.

They swarm, a mass,
Oblivious to the call of war,
Back to coaches, cars and bikes.

I stand alone
My comrades fall around me
The stench of death surrounds me.

Fog slides along the early morning ground
Obliterating the footsteps of my passage
Across the expanse.

I am alone
Fields stretch for miles where once
I fought and died.

I stand alone
The fighting ceased, peace restored
As I visit the battlefield
Lest we forget!

Josephine Marks

BATTLEFIELDS

And I saw the dead lying there,
Their open eyes more piercing in their sightlessness.
Their open mouths more loud in their silence.
Their multitude expounding the failure,
Of the politicians who sent them there.

David Evans

A LAND FIT FOR HEROES

In a land fit for heroes
What did they fight for?
And in a land fit for heroes
What did they live for?
Generals receiving thousands
For the death of a generation
Soldiers a few shillings
For a wound or two

Find yourself a job
And fight for your rights
And we'll end your shift
With a scribe of a pen
Like a sickle on corn
A scythe of the gun
Men fall
As the dole queue grows and grows

The factory of the valley
Has closed
What did they tell our grandparents
As they grew up
Finding food to fill
A mother's breast
This great empire
Of promises
Of promises

Aled Hughes

11 SEPTEMBER 2001

I was with my mother,
on my way to school.
A plane roared overhead,
Mother stopped the car.

Then all was confusion -
the tall tower crashed down
with horrendous noise.
My mother held me close,
shielding me with her body.
A massive slab of masonry
crashed through the car roof
hitting Mother on her head,
and she lay still.

We are exhorted -
'Forgive your enemies,
bless your persecutors.'
But how?

Our faceless enemy
killed himself.
But ultimately -
who was to blame?

Avenge my mother I cannot.
I ask God to help me.
May God forgive you,
whoever you are.
For I cannot . . .

Maria-Christina

ALL QUIET ON THE CEMETERY FRONT
(For the Wednesbury Arts Festival 2002)

Eugenic from an industrial womb
Bust my dear home, Wednesbury.
Basking in the Pax Britannic noon
The town hummed and soon,
Exemplified progress for all to see:
Yet the early start, the economic tomb.

Sun in the heavens, Black Country beneath,
Belching forth the furnaces of Wednesbury.
Britannia, the heir of Rome the belief,
Smiling smugly with grimy teeth
At the turn of the twentieth century;
Her sons would be spent as funeral wreaths.

The Co-op Grandad Degville once built
Remains cornering Union Street, Wednesbury.
His town's flower, at Flanders wilt;
While Britannia, her crown was tilt:
And again, at Ypres, another muddy sea
To slink away, clutching bloody pelts.

People weep beneath cenotaph-choked stones
For their misspent heroes of Wednesbury.
Wives and little children were left all alone,
To mourn their daddies' rain-bleached bones
Strewn in a shell-streaked mortuary.
Has that imperial sun really gone down?

Now all is still, except the cemetery mower,
The only sound in redundant Wednesbury.
Young men wasted, we cannot sink any lower:
But caressed by life's sun and showers,
New life and energy there shall be
Where the scythe dares not hover.

Epilogue

Take a walk; every building tells its story,
Piled high in the Land of Hope and Glory;
Stashed obituaries high, 'Lest we forget'
Flanders' poppies on which the imperial sun set.

Ian D Henery

THE CHILDREN

Only six but they know the hell
Of rifle shots and exploding shell.
They always have the same clothes on,
The shops are burnt down
Where they come from.

Lost their toys
And friends, girls and boys.
Their father gone away.
Mother please tell them.
They ask
When will they leave this cellar
They call home each day?

Mother will tell them
Father will be home very soon.
Then they will have their own big room
With all new books set upon the shelves.
New clothes they will have
Chocolate and sweets, teddies and elves.

When then will Daddy come home?
Mummy please can you tell?
The mother bites her lip
For she knows
It all depends on the bullet and shell.

Frederick Seymour

TRIBUTE

The horizontal rain deluged from barren ground, not sky
It severed the air like the polished blade of a thousand samurai
Relentless hail poured forth, bestowing its poor man's accolade
Conferring bloody knighthood with each soothing drop, man had made
He lay flat against the hot earth, breathless, and wiped away the sweat
And asked, 'How can I stand in all this rain and not get wet?'

The leaves around exploded in viridian confetti, flickered
                                                            then blew away
Some took purchase on his shoulder, though this was not
                                                            his wedding day
Yet so many best men to choose from each in protection of a ring
In poverty cast to fit the finger but attached to a safety pin
He stared calmly at the fragments and brushed them from his epaulette
And thought, how could it rain on your wedding day and you
                                                            don't get wet?

And if it were, would he have his witness, someone left to say
To testify that these young men stood side by side this day
As they marched the narrow aisle, herd trodden by cattle feet
A mosaic of elephantiasis mud, baked hard by sun and heat
No floral tributes placed before this regal march, not yet
Time enough for flowers, so many earthen beds back home to let.

No organ player for the wedding march, just the loud tattoo of gun
Pounding out like a fearful heart that's work was almost done
As it beat the time with the marching feet of this stately entourage
Who so proudly displayed their uniforms, daubed with camouflage
But their given pledge the shilling taken, now thought of with regret
For how could it rain so heavily and not one of them get wet?

The trees, nature's forms lay empty, no life, no birds in song
With the wisdom to desert had taken flight, long since freedom born
Then one single drop of rain did what a million had not done
As it fell upon the breast of yet another mother's son
This one red drop of man-made rain traced his brother Vet
He held the soldier in his arms and cried,
'How can it rain on so many men and not one of us get wet?'

Liam Fyffe

PEACE

I stood to watch the water lilies
As still they lay upon the pond
Ivory petals shone in sunshine
Felt my heart to them respond

Still and silent is the water,
As my gaze spreads far and wide.
Nature paints a brilliant picture -
All is peace personified.

In the twilight of the evening,
Memories flood my heart and mind,
See again those water lilies
As about my heart they twine.

All their beauty, and their splendour
Once again my vision sees.
Nature gives this tranquil beauty,
Lets my lonely heart perceive.

So often we don't realise
When 'peace' invades the heart,
How precious is the picture
That the inner eye imparts.

M Gibson

CONFLICT

A peaceful place would be Utopia, especially in our present world
Where everyone is convinced their beliefs are right
And all the others wrong
Or that the 'grass is greener' so will fight and kill to reach it
Whilst teaching that peace would be better, quieter, more harmonious
And war would be worth suffering to prove that point!
War is a small word but causes massive disharmony and unhappiness
Suffering, mayhem and death heedless of creed or age
Too deaf to hear the pitiful screams of those who are lost
Media coverage relays news to far-flung relatives
Aware their loved ones are in the war-torn lands
Unsure of who's fighting whom, why there's so much hatred.
But, Lord, there are still those people who pray for peace
Knowing it's a perpetual cry, ignoring the ones convinced they're right
Families and friends torn apart through their different beliefs
But we continue to pray for peace to vanquish the never-ending wars
And honour the many selfless acts of heroism within the chaos.

Tilla B Smith

SOMEWHERE A CANDLE GLOWS

Life ebbs into the dawn
and an emptiness
echoes the weeping,
gently borne on breezes lifting
hate in billowing clouds
and time stands still in sorrow's reaping.

Teardrops glisten dust,
chase memories, shivering the
numbness of a day made senseless,
life and love scorched
into earth, no more is laughter
heard and all is lifeless.

Love waits in vigil wearily,
searches despair in debris
twisted shattered in repose,
life's sanctity ridiculed tossed
away, then faith finds love and
somewhere in the dark, a candle glows.

Lorna Troop

MESSAGE FOR 2001
(Luke 21 verses 20-22)

The city is surrounded the tanks are at the gate
Bloodshed at every corner, the call 'exterminate'.
From many camps and nations fanatics fail to see
That every act of violence will stand eternally.

They suffocate compassion and stifle common-sense
Reap malice for the children, a grim inheritance,
The hatred of the ages with men of war returns,
No tenderness in these eyes where only vengeance burns.

The prophet calls the people to listen to the Word
But in tumultuous hatred reason is never heard.
Mankind can never listen to people sore oppressed
They look through narrow windows where everyone is blessed.

Grim warnings through the ages yet proud men never learn
The need for all to listen, and old ways overturn.
This tit for tat destruction steals life and touches all
Can no voice plead compassion to end this senseless brawl?

Each thinks they are God's chosen and yet ignore His will,
In every man's instruction, the words 'Thou shalt not kill'!
Oh God, send Light to guide us, for darkness is at hand
We need the promised teacher that *all* can understand.

E Kronbergs

WAR (PART 2)

Just a three-letter word,
Yet it is the cause of
So much heartache and pain.

Two world wars,
And many other acts of pointless violence.
Millions have died, maybe more
In just a hundred years.

It doesn't matter why it started,
Life is too precious to throw away
Over land or religion.

The innocent die
While politicians sit in their offices.
They take all the credit
While the soldiers die.
So what's the point?
There are no winners,
Just losers
In that three-letter word.

Corwin Barber

AFTERMATH AFRICA

Their bodies line the track
four and five deep
as far as the eye can see
many are already dead
decomposed and stinking
in the heat
covered in swarms of sated
buzzing flies
    there are no rats
    they were eaten long ago.

A few still live
bare skeletons
with skin that scarcely covers bone
massed with running sores
too weak to move
their agonised brilliant eyes
still plead in hope
    for the love of God
    please help us
    please help our children.

Joan Briggs

NEWSFLASH

In between the television news
And what's running in the three o'clock,
A far away war raged on innocents
The flash was short, made to shock.
She clutched her baby to her breast
While pleading for her life,
Her man lay headless in the dust
Her crime, she was his wife.
The steel cut keen across the babe
And she fell to her knees,
Was raped and then raped again
The soldiers deaf to her pleas.
The smell of death was all around
Yet no tear did she shed,
For now her fight was over
No more in blood to tread.
Does this brashly crush youth's tender cords
Of what are dreams and what is destiny?
While tinged with fear we talk of compassion
When we truly feel and not just see.

J M Rosson Gaskin

A Night In The Life

Hair's breadth they say
between genius and madness
as hand in hand
walk love and sadness

Hair's breadth bad day
between love and hate
best understood by those
who co-habitate

This does not go
by the numbers
kind remarks
flying tumblers

Passionate relations
heavy frustrations
broken down
communications

Love eternal
sweet and dear
keep it down
the neighbours will hear

We have to be all
we seem to be
mind your manners
five o'clock for tea

Little Red Riding Hood
has come out to play
for all the wolves
have gone away

As the dust settles down
on another day.

Greig Hepson

SEPTEMBER MORN

Twin towers stood so proud and tall
Sentinels in a wealthy land,
A country's heart, a mighty power
A clock which beat with steady hand.

One day in autumn clear and bright
That heart was torn and lost from sight,
And now they stand no longer tall
A mass of iron and bricks that fall.

Those blackened ashes cried in vain
For help to lift that awful pain.
Such grief, such loss, an ache so deep
That men could only stand and weep.

Then silence came across that land
Encircled like an iron band,
Drawn faces etched across the sky
A million voices asking 'W*hy?*'

So stirred a rage of ancient fires
To burn like Hell's eternal pyres
Old Nemesis returned on wings
To rid the world of evil things.

The hunt is on, will justice reign
For those who bear the mark of Cain?
That settled dust, those silent tears
Bear witness down the coming years.

Give grace and strength to all who mourn
And courage to whose lives were torn,
A hope, a prayer, that men find peace
This world is only ours on lease.

Ruth Terry

THE TELEGRAM

A moth fluttered dangerously closer and closer to the naked flame of the candle, then in a second lay crumpled and lifeless at its base. The old man, sitting by the fire, stared at the envelope in his hand, afraid to open it. Then, on reading that his only son had been killed in action on the Somme, he let out a great cry of anguish, and, like the moth, he too was no more. Suddenly the dark room was filled with light. 'Billy,' cried the old man with joy, and father and son embraced. Outside, the wind began to moan and a draught of cold air swept through the oak-beamed room. The fire no longer glowed in the old stone fireplace, and the solitary candle flickered twice, and finally went out.

Diane Berthelot

WAR AND PEACE

You are angry with me
I am angry with me
Saying things that weren't meant to be
Round and round in circles
Circles of hate, love and anger
Rotating with no thought of time
Passions engulf and consume us
Mocking at our distress
Enjoying our anger
Provoking more thunder
A storm of tears
Droplets then torrents
Warming winds of thought
Calm and soothe us
Time slows
With Mother Nature taking care
And Father Time forgiving
For wasting his.

Karen Disney

WAR CHILD

Bombs exploding everywhere.
Those murdering soldiers just don't care.
This terrified child, has no hiding place.
With tears in her eyes, running down her face.
Six years old, she is just a tot.
As she cries for her parents, after they were shot.
She said Mummy and Daddy are both sleeping.
But I can't wake them up, as she sat there weeping.
One soldier looked down feeling really bad.
After killing the only precious things, this little girl had.
With a lump in his throat. He tried to explain.
But nothing he said could cure her pain.
The little girl looked in disarray.
After the soldier got up and walked away.
She was left alone, still full of tears,
With no mummy and daddy, for the rest of her years.

Stephen Hibbeler

WHY?

So dreadful this world in which we dwell,
Filled with an evil too great to tell.
Our hearts so heavy with the horrendous sights,
The shocking nightmares which numb our nights.
How can we convey to victims our sadness and our grief?
Or the depth of our outrage, which goes beyond belief?
We can only offer our arms to comfort and embrace,
Offer our support for the tomorrows that they face.
Hold on to the thought that one day there will be peace,
And pray for a brighter future where all hostilities cease.
Sometimes faith in the future is the only way to cope,
And remember that in Pandora's box there remained only hope.

Angela Burse

JUST A DREAM

Among the graves in serried rows
The autumn wind more strongly blows,
And leaves now turned to russet gold
At last release their fragile hold,
Then blown to the ground or into a ditch
They make the earth more humus rich.

But when the withering winds of war
Blew down young men like leaves or straw,
Into the earth they then were laid
In rows as though still on parade.
The withering winds of dreadful war
Blew them from the 'tree of life' before
Their full span of life had run
That wind a rifle, shell or gun.

Above them stands a stone of whitish grey
Where their loved ones may one day pray,
Some have no name upon their stone
Their names are known to God alone;
But do their remains the earth enrich
Like leaves decaying in a ditch?

The grass around their graves is short and neat
Where we can walk with quiet feet,
And as we pass in silent thought
We think what gain has their death brought?
That statesmen could have found with arbitration
To spare the grief of many a nation;
But evil men still plot and scheme
A peaceful world is just a dream.

Roy Dickinson

WAR

She tabled sheets of stocks and sales,
And profit/loss per items sold,
All neatly ranged in ranks and rows.
She then observed, with false lament,
Our prices need to be increased.
But softy spoken man, she thought
Of little worth, addressed the chair.
He quietly undermined the sums
Per units shown, revealing flaws
In underlying bases used
That varied right across the spread.
The rustled papers, scratch of heads
Of others right and left, now showed
They'd not considered figures thus.
The chairman gave assent to view
We need the facts, not lies, before
Decisions can be made. And so
Reprieve achieved for time a chance
To put a rival case. But she
Who'd fudged accounts was boiling mad
With anger's hidden rage. She smiled
At one and all and pleaded weight
Of work had led to minor faults
In database she'd used in haste.
Beneath synthetic charm she seethed
At loss of face and vowed revenge.
It's thus a secret war began.
It's thus that nations find themselves
In clash of arms without a cause
That merits killing mums and kids.

Henry Disney

WAR AND PEACE

'England and its dependants, should now freely unite into an ongoing independent nation, free from European laws, for we made the world what it is, we gave them their independence back, for do we really want more trouble upon our own backyard, we need to govern ourselves, let's not complicate things even more that they are at present.'

'An indolent mind will always become a wayward one, but with time, it might become a pleasanter one'

'Mankind's archaic nature is still very obvious, he still kills his own kind which obviously is degrading'

'Philosophical, God is on all our sides, he does not pick and choose'

'What gives a man the right to kill another human being? He has no right'

'Ethnic cleansing is a poor man's notion of a better world'

'To grumble continuously is to grumble at one's own expense'

'The Palestinians should have their land returned to them, with proper respect shown on both sides then there will be peace, one cannot take away from the other and expect the situation to be resolved, for in reality it never shall'

'The different factions throughout the world who kill, maim, bomb, should lay down their arms and inspire their communities with beautiful conceptions, instead of creating continual fear and hatred amongst themselves, for God did not expect you to kill your brother man, nothing can become of it but further hatred, loss of life, and tears that stain the land'

'Why cause so much destruction and death upon others, when you could be constructing a better world for yourselves and your neighbours? It seems so foolish in the first place, to wantonly destroy what was once beautiful'

'Mighty is the man or woman who truly knows of the truth within'

'Philosophy should be continually analysed throughout, for further truths shall overtake past reflections upon its ancient path for better insight and learning, for mankind's upward struggle and progress.'

James Stephen Cameron

WAR AND PEACE

Why is there war?
What's there to gain?
Apart from bloodshed, hatred and pain

Why do we fight
With our loved ones and friends?
A waste of emotions when we make amends

Why do we shout
With such anger and noise?
When it's better we're calm, have decorum and poise

Why do we frown
When a smile is so warm?
We cause our own anguish - an internal storm

Where is the laughter
Instead of the duels?
And the passion for life, that peacefulness fuels

Where is the peace
In our hearts and our world?
There is always some stone that seems to be hurled

Where are we heading?
No one can say
For now, life is for living - we should cherish each day

Susanne Semmence

WAR

Here they come, it's the sound of a plane,
I glanced at her face and saw the blood drain.
Then the explosion and people screaming,
why can't I move, am I dreaming?

Suddenly my memory's returning,
and I'm aware of something burning.
I can turn my head, that's a relief,
then I'm staring in disbelief.
This was our home, now all I can see
is dust and smoke and flying debris.

Then I'm shouting 'Where are you my love?'
and I find myself praying to the good Lord above.
To think the unthinkable I couldn't abide,
I wouldn't want to live without her at my side.

Suddenly I hear her voice, although it's not clear
I can make out the words, 'I'm alright and you sound quite near,
but what about you, are you ok? I will try to reach you, if I can
just find my way.'
Then her hand is in mine and we embrace,
as we kiss I can feel her tears on my face.

How long we lay there I have no idea,
but we were together so we didn't feel fear.
How did it begin? It seems so long ago,
politicians talking then we're bombed by NATO.

R S Hooper

WORLD CONFLICTS

When will these conflicts end? I pray, there is no response
When will peace prevail and put an end to all these wants?
When will nations agree and set this poor old world to right?
How wonderful just dreaming about it. Lord have you all in sight?
This beautiful orb you created, how disappointed you must be
To see continual bloodshed for so-called faith and liberty.
We intercede continually, make there a lasting peace
Let there be no further hostility, make all these conflicts cease.

Of they great understanding as we have read in days of old
Where plagues and many misfortunes, so these tales are told
By your hand they perished, revealing one true light
Creating man in your own being, help now to put all right
The suffering and the torment, the grief and continual pain
As men face men with awesome tools, bless them in Thy name.
Surely it is not your wish to see little children maimed
Brothers and sisters face the firing squad, this surely was not ordained?

Mothers weep, fathers are demented, aged parents killed and gone
Where once happy, contented families, do they now in heaven belong?
Boy soldiers brainwashed into action in the name of God
Only to be destroyed, now called martyrs, buried in the sod
We, pleading, entreat Thee make those in authority see sense
Not destroying many great nations, the ones you designed and invent
Please make thy might shine in those war lords' eyes
Let us return to continued peace and a world of paradise.

R D Hiscoke

RISE UP

Rise up, rise up from the ground
From the ashes scattered around
Intense burning, fiery heat
Has corroded and melted every street.

Buildings no long stand tall
A catastrophic event has made them fall
They once heralded throngs of occupants
Now all have gone, lives have been spent.

Sunlight flickers slightly through the dark mist
As a man stands bewildered, clenching his fist
A sickly silence has settled amongst the few
Who survived. But why? If only they knew.

Those who are left bury the dead
Was this their biggest fear, biggest dread?
An act of God or an act of tyranny?
Whatever the outcome, they have the world's sympathy.

What was once a very, very proud race
Now bitter, have to put on a brave face.
To rise up, rebuild, to become so much stronger
For this day, they cannot forget any longer.

Chris Ward

FAREWELL TO ARMS

'Charge for the guns! Forward, the Light Brigade!'
(Last night I dreamed Love lured me to her bed,
With soft white arms, and silken tressèd head).
Heed not the shot; orders must be obeyed.
Though volleys roar, trust to the naked blade!
(Upon the sheet the virgin flower blushed red.
What though before tomorrow I be dead,
Last night, my love - oh, the wild charge we made!)

Hearts' hoof beats pounding, hell for leather, leap
The redoubt; drive home each thrilling sabre-thrust,
Daring the cannon's mouth which, jarring deep,
Ejaculates its full Vulcanic lust -
A brief transfiguration, searing white -
Then, in the dark of death, scream for the light!

Bernard Brown

WAR AND PEACE

The terrorism that affects the world today
Causes the destruction, in a pathetic way
Innocent people that have lost their lives
Those that have lost loved ones, children, husbands and wives.

We shall always remember the 11th of September
The shock, the tragedy, of the twin towers
The heartache, the screams, in New York city
The shock of it all, the suicidal tragedy.

Still war goes on in Palestine, affecting the innocent
The suffering, the ignorance of the people and terrible incident
Even to dress a young child, with bombs and ammunition
Teaching a child their ways of wickedness and destruction.

Will there ever be peace in Ireland? We shall never understand
Fighting through their beliefs, politics, their land
Could there ever be a compromise, or have things gone too far?
Would there ever be peace, whatever religion they are?

We can always rebuild the land again
But innocent people will always suffer through
Terrorism, blood and endless pain.
Let's hope one day there will be
Peace and hope, throughout each country.

Jean McGovern

WAR AND PEACE

What a horrid and torrid world we live in,
People are not friendly any more,
Now there are conflicts and wars,
All around the world today,
There's even troubles outside our doors,

Yet we've begun to live with it,
Because we had lost our way,
For whoever governs over us,
Don't give a damn of what we say,

We were sold down the river
Such a long, long time ago,
Whether Tony Blair or Maggie Thatcher,
They're all the same, you must now know.

Now that Blair is Bush's right-hand man,
Soon we could be in the land of the free,
Or if we're not very careful,
It may be the start of World War III.

What has happened to those carefree days,
When people said 'Hello' and a bit more than cheerio?
The '50s, '60s and the '70s I loved best,
Tell you something for nothing,
It'll put these years to the test.

And it's not getting any better,
You can see it for yourself,
It's in all of the tabloids,
I know, it has affected my health.

Now that we're in Europe,
We have to do as we are told,
Don't worry about your pensions,
You won't get it, now that you've been sold.

B Mitchell

PEACE IN NORTHERN IRELAND

Peace in Northern Ireland
Is a sight I'd like to see
There's no need for all this conflict
It's a disgrace if you ask me.

The Peace Process it came to light
But peace I've yet to see
Don't get me wrong, things have calmed down
But aren't as calm as they could be.

Still many people lose their lives
Or are injured in some way
By blast bombs or in shootings
That are happening each day.

If only everyone would stop
And take the time to see
That although we have our differences
We could live in harmony.

Who we are as individuals
Should never pose a threat
It's a thing we should be proud of
And not a thing that we regret.

I really hope that things will change
And the killings will all cease
That people throughout Ireland
Could somehow live in peace.

If people really wanted peace
Then peace is what they'd get
But peace in Northern Ireland
Has a long way to go yet.

J L Preston

What Peace?

When peace broke out, we ran about, two fingers in the air
Making 'V' for victory signs and flowers in our hair.
We knew the score 'Make love, not war' is what we used to sing
But now we know it just ain't so. It didn't mean a thing!
The lads came home across the foam. Heroes every one,
Except for those we left behind beneath the Rising Sun.
My old pal Jack, he made it back. He was a broken man.
Used for bayonet practice by the 'heroes' of Japan.
His blood was shed. He was left for dead.
To see him you'd have cried.
He just said 'Hello Mother,' poor b*****d, then he died.
60 years on. All hope is gone. But memories remain,
We can't forget the torture and still we feel the pain.
Malaria-ridden British rats, caged in Changi jail,
We slaved upon that railway and weren't allowed to fail.
We built a bridge for b*****ds across the River Kwai
And thousands of our comrades were left out there to die,
Christ said 'Love your enemies' but how can I do that?
Whenever I see a yellow man, I want to knock him flat.
For some the memories are gone.
But as for me, *the war's still on!*

Norman Chandler

War And Peace

Calamity and calm go hand in hand
With danger, on the fearsome plain of war.
One plot with many characters on stage,
Gunfire and illusion, the backdrop's deadly flaw.
Headlong the aspirations hurl aside the doubts
Battle lines are blurred, no heroes left to care.
Sublimated strategies, hopes forever dashed
As explosive acclamations fill the air.

Performers weary, destitute, the drama almost done,
The hierarchy of orders fills the breach.
Unravelling plots in ruins, anticipation gone,
Costume bedecked players fall silent one by one.
Exhilarating dreams are dead and silence fills the air,
Life enhancing peace is left for all around to share.

N Rudge

ONLY NEWS

Oh what a wonderful world
we live in,
guns ablazing,
blood flying.

Oh what a wonderful world,
to be born into,
orphaned babies,
woman and children murdered,
under the jewel-encrusted sun.

Oh what a wonderful world,
to live in,
hungry, our stomachs sag,
over crumbly bones,
exposed and vulnerable.

Oh what a wonderful world,
to die in,
all the bloodshed,
tarnishing silver swords,
marinating the triggers of guns,
masking invaders against truth and justice.
Oh what a wonderful world,
are you enjoying the show?

Michelle Landon

TESTOSTERONE

Across their arid borders face two nations bent on war.
In 60 years or maybe less the world will ask 'What for?
Did empty tracts of desert land so fill you with desire
That you would give your life and sons to quench your pointless ire?'

Both nations thought quite long and hard about their future fight.
Their wise men carried on while others went home for the night.
Some died while thinking, some lived on, but answer there was none
But we know that it's down to our old friend *testosterone!*

Two boys are out a-drinking and they see one pretty girl.
Before they know what's hit them both their minds are in a whirl.
Both want her so but both must know what's in the other's mind.
The one who is the loser is the one who stays behind.

And so they fight and blood soon flows. One's cut above the eye
But they are being men of course, and so the fur must fly!
Though she's long gone along the street, they fight till ten past one
And underneath the reason is again *testosterone!*

This nasty little hormone drives all folk but it's silent.
It fires imaginations but only if they're violent.
It lives in every one of us, in women and in men
And every time it surfaces its anger we must pen.
When first you feel it rising find a little stick to bite on -
If we cannot subdue it then there'll be no world to fight on!

Lesley S Robinson

THE POWER OF THE WORLD

A world of misguided deceit
Human - murder - Arafat -
Bin Laden in another league
Or even Bush and Blair
Who really dares to stare
In the children's faces?

Powerful men in their own ways
Their opinion is the only view
Taking the inferior
Ordinary people wiped away
They all can be guilty in some way
Power is very addictive
Be careful
Why?
Think before you speak.

E A Triggs

WAR AND PEACE

'Darling! I love you. Tell the kids I love them too. I think
we are going to die!' (Silence! Nothing!)
'Hallo, hallo, (Honey hallo).'
'Mummy, was that Daddy?'
I see, I hear, I don't believe,
People screaming, smoke everywhere, I hear people shouting,
'My God! Did you see that plane?'
Are all those people going to die in vain?
Someone drags me down the street,
I can't see, I just cannot see.
Please God, don't let this be.
Am I dreaming? I think I am screaming.
The second plane hits, my blood turns cold but it still drips.
The Tower is coming down, I see people falling to the ground.
Is it night, or is it day? The smell of death is all around.
Sirens, sirens, noise, dirt, shouting and crying.
People lying on the floor, gaping wounds that can be treated no more!
My thoughts are hazy, I try to remember.
But all I know for sure is that the world will never forget
This September!

Janet Marie Lord

11TH OF SEPTEMBER

11th of September -
Was the day that changed the world
And the terror of the terrorists
Was cruelly unfurled.
But the courage of the fire-fighters
Became a force supreme
And out of all the misery
Came a radiant gleam.
United in their grief and fear
They faced a world unknown
When evil struck and horror reigned
When men and women mown.
Strong men wept and mothers cried
When they saw their sons had died,
Sacrifice and deeds of love
Where shown that fateful day.
For higher forces rule the world
And goodness will held sway,
Then like a phoenix from the ashes
Of the Trade Center of the world
Rose the crosses of the structure
From which people had been hurled.
The cross stands high and God will reign
Throughout a world bereft of pain.
Bad will be banished, shadows gone
Comes hope and joy where the cross has shone.

11th of November - was the day that war did cease
11th of September - God grant a pact of peace.

Mollie D Earl

LOVE THY NEIGHBOUR

An eye for an eye is a dangerous game,
hurt someone and they'll hurt you the same
Innocent blood sometimes they spill,
the name of the game is kill for kill.
Traps are set but don't take the bait,
don't get caught up in hate for hate.
Take the heat out of the fire,
Israelis and Palestinians love thy neighbour.

Some laws say kill and you'll be killed,
a life for a life, the law is fulfilled.
If you kill you'll go to prison,
the law's revenge, your life will be taken.
Governments and terrorists fight for the thrill,
tit for tat they kill for kill.
Take the heat out of the fire,
Serbians and Kosovans love thy neighbour.

Religious groups and races draw your brakes,
stop giving your neighbours headaches.
Are you addicted to the violence pill?
Why die for the game kill for the kill?
Violence creates problems, it never gets sorted,
revenge takes you back to where it started.
Chechens and Russians cease and settle,
no more wars, no more battle.
The same goes for Serbs, Muslims and Croats,
stop fighting each other like dogs and cats.
Let us all shake hands and help each other,
you will have peace if you love your neighbour.

Barrington Delevante

BRAVEHEARTS

Stagnant mist hung in the air,
and the glens were dank and sodden.
That morning of the 16th,
when the English took Culloden.

The Highlands soon fell silent,
like they had never done before.
When the clans all joined together,
for this bloody civil war.

Bagpipes proudly boasted
of the battle yet to come.
The English troops replied,
with bugle and with drum.

The outnumbered clans attacked,
with passion and with pride.
But grape-shot, cannon and musketry,
halted the marauding tide.

With the Jacobite cause in ruins,
and the Bonnie Prince on the run.
The 'butcher' Duke of Cumberland,
announced the battle won.

Will the pain of Scotland ever heal,
or change the way her people feel?
Or does the memory burn too deep,
so as ye sow, then ye shall reap?

Allan Wood

WAR AND PEACE

Terror is what Israelis see,
Occupation stops Palestinians being free.
Israelis feel terror all around
So they occupy Palestinian ground.

An unimaginative stalemate
Small shifts in awareness
The good people work for tolerance, fairness,
Fear and dread blight the brain.
Ethnically similar
They should finish the pain.

Change can flow from those involved
Emphatic acts to get things resolved.
That's the crux and that's the core.
Time to let go of keeping the score.
Two singing peoples who also dance.
Their children's futures left to chance.

To enrich their minds
The time must come
When Israelis and Palestinians
Share the golden dome.
A sanctuary, their inclusive home.

Hug, drink tea in each other's house
End the years of 'cat and mouse'.

Carol Sherwood

STEP BACK FROM THE BRINK

Wake up - India and Pakistan - you've plunged the world
                                                    in a nightmare!
    Ape not the fascist despots, Adolf and Benito, the viley pair!
Search the labyrinths of your conscience - be not blind to
                                                    your own folly,
    Surmount your sore Kashmir impasse, mutually and amicably -
Phantoms of Hiroshima and Nagasaki still haunt the human mind,
    And Chernobyl's reactor explosion doth, of Hades, remind!
Should sane restraints on you both, (obsessed with super-nukes)
                                                    fail to act,
    All point to a looming apocalyptic revengeful tit-for-tat,
Ponder ye - what would happen if either pushed the button, anon
    To fire the 'Ghauri ballistic missile' by Moslem Pakistan,
Or the matching 'Agni MK2 missiles' by Hindu India,
    With no U-turn - but horrendous nuke-carnage in this vendetta.
This is not the end: it's not even the beginning of the end!
    Maybe, it's the end of the beginning - with no warning sent,
The 'Ghauri' would have exploded 800 feet above Delhi,
    And, in retaliation, three 'Agni MK2 missiles' would blitz Karachi!
The missiles will vaporise in vast fireballs hotter than the sun,
    Millions dead, or gravely injured - with chunks of burning
                                            flesh, - on the run,
Thousands blinded by atomic flash and gama radiation,
    Stagger, needing doctors, nurses, rescue workers, and sanitation,
Radioactive fallout could reach Britain, as after Chernobyl -
    Ground water contaminated would put populace in peril -
Monsoons would carry fallout to countries not involved in the conflict,
    And the biological impact on men and beasts - catastrophic,
Oppenheimer's creation - the atom bomb - 'unleashed death,
                                                  the destroyer' -

He then reminisced this quote from the Hindu 'Bhagavad -
Gita' scripture -
Brothers of India and Pakistan, make peace and be reconciled,
The Nation with courage to make the first move,
Wins the World War III in style!

Welch Jeyaraj Balsingam

THE BUTTON

How futile it must be
When two great nations
Go to war in the air, land and sea
What for? Nobody knows
As they kill each other with mortal blows.

Through the years there is suffering
Through the years there is much pain
Then someone signs a treaty
And peace is proclaimed.

No one knows how long for
These great nations again go to war
But some bright spark invented the bomb
All the great nations greeted this with great aplomb.

Then they all took a different view
When they saw the destruction these bombs could do
Now they are afraid to go to war
For life on Earth will be no more
Maybe fate had something to do with the bomb
Because the threat of war I think has gone
The terrorist nut I have not forgotten
He could bring about Armageddon

Bert Booley

WAR

Marching, marching through the land,
Through rain, through snow and desert sand.

Blood and bodies increasing at an alarming rate,
To be killed by bullets, is the soldier's fate.

No heart or mind, but that of stone,
The King of Peace has been overthrown.

As strong as we are united, as weak as we are alone,
What if we'd realised what we have known?

For the workers of this evil, death is but a chore,
But all we know is, this is the start of war.

Emotions cast away, feelings cast aside,
The enemy has been attempting what we can't abide.

A last idea, thought a soldier as he died,
We have to win, because God is on our side.

But God can't be with everyone, of that we can be sure,
In fact God is not on any side, as he does not believe in war.

If they had ditched their hatred, and evil been above,
War would not be in the dictionary, instead there would be love.

Siôn Griffiths

INNOCENT VICTIMS

On 11th September the world stood still,
when some evil fools set out to kill.
They were sent by a coward so low,
from another country where we don't go.
The heartless fools hijacked a plane,
and shot the pilot, these men were insane.

They flew them into the Twin Towers that once stood up high,
also The Pentagon as smoke filled the sky.
Many tears and broken hearts,
and lots of families torn apart.
Clouds of smoke so people couldn't see,
could this be the beginning of World War Three?

Sophie Trenchard

HOW MANY HANDS ROCK THE CRADLE?

Hunger strike, Loyalist strike
Dirty war, take a hike
2002. 3,000 and more
Very nearly peace galore.

Adams, Hume, Trimble, Mallon;
Trimble, Durkan, this thing, it's workin'
Devolved power, people power
Cometh the men, cometh the hour.

Belfast daily up in smoke
Morally bankrupt, emotionally broke.
In a warped sort of way, it must be said,
An argument for another day.

Cash is flowing, houses are selling
Old people's homes, on deals they're welching
Homelessness, it shows no favour,
Whether coming from or going to your saviour.

Why do we dwell on days gone by?
Always the same indifferent cry
Looking forward may be hard,
Hopefully a future we won't discard.

Tim Frogman

THE SNOWS ARE STILL MELTING

Who will remember - who can forget?
Father forgive we have sinned.
Furnaces burning deep into the night,
Lives blown away in the wind.

They came in their thousands their lives in a case,
The rich and the poor all from one race.
Doctors or farmers, their future the same,
With questioning eyes - who is to blame?

Herded in ghettos so easy to find,
Still unbelieving, their senses still blind.
Loaded on wagons packed in like sheep,
Winter or summer, the sky has to weep.

'Where are my children?' a voice in the storm,
The veil in the temple is suddenly torn.
Monsters in uniforms shiny and smart,
Have blinded the world and ripped out its heart.

Many years later the world still looks back,
Desperately trying to cover its tracks.
'We're not to blame - we did not know,'
Still the furnaces are melting the snow.

All over the world innocents die,
While masked killers spread the world's greatest lie.
'This is God's will!' But they'll never know.
At the coming of spring their cause will melt with the snow.

Africa -Asia - go where you will,
The uniformed monsters are still out to kill.
Father forgive, we all have sinned,
For lives are still blown away in the wind.

WJFH

WAR AND PEACE

The futility of war planned by man's
Greed to play games with people's lives.
The ego boosting politicians
With their senseless acts
Spare little thought for those torn apart
Often than not the heart is
          Ripped
                Stripped
                        From a family

Who will dry their tears?
Or fill the years of empty spaces?
Who really wins in the end?

Is it the enemies?
                The oppressors?
                      The dictators?
Who hide in their safe burrows
These men of war raging habits
Who only show their faces in the light of glory
Another story
              At the expense of the innocent

Have they no conscience?
How do they know what's best?

Peaceful solutions can show the way
Only peace extends its hand to all

No matter what colour or creed
All people should have the right to live
In harmony with their fellow man.

Eileen Kyriacou

THE ANGUISH LIVES ON

It was quiet in the village before the soldiers came,
the church bells tolled and called us all to prayer.
A gentle flow of worshippers plodded down the street.
But her family weren't believers and did not respond to it.

She wondered as she stared through the broken windowpane,
why God had let this happen and left them all alone.
Was he really up there . . . did he really care?
She turned to her brother sobbing on the stair.

Her thoughts were numbed, her recollections blurred,
all she could remember was the screaming she had heard.
Grandma's voice echoed through her mind:
'Quick, hide everybody, the soldiers are here.'

Down the street they had stormed and broken down the door.
Next she had heard the gunshots as she slithered to the floor.
It seemed hours before she had dared to stir and
to crawl out from her hiding place.

Shaken and frightened she crept down the stairs
to find her grandma face down and still.
She touched her granny's hand to find some comfort
but it was cold and blue . . .

Next she found her mother, blood dried upon her face,
her body limp and lifeless, sprawled across the yard.
Father was gone and they'd taken Marco too.
She was all alone and knew not what to do.

But then she heard a whisper, uttered like a prayer:
'Can I come out now . . . is there anybody there?
Where's Mummy . . . is she okay?'
It was little brother Carlos, just five years old that day.

He crawled from beneath his bed.
She shuddered as she saw the terror in his face.
He hugged her and clung to her, stunned by disbelief.
No words exchanged, just a sharing of their grief.

Eve McGrath

ENTER THE DRAGON

He was never killed only his shadow.
As ever he heaves and seethes in his den
and bubbles in the hearts of men,
his red eyes searching out the arteries of hate.

He is never short of parasites in need of bile
to feed their envious and hateful blood.
Never a shortage in the land of sick shepherds
rounding up the scapegoats to feed their master.

From icy polar waste to the tropics of Hades
scorching his careful path with outriders
in white cowl and black pyjama
with orange sash and balaclava
he slimes and creeps and climbs to breach
the walls of decency and order raised against him.

The tempests of his coming reach to blow away
the frail webs woven in care and beauty
to shield the nests of the young,
and save the treasure.

His qualified captains, paid up members
of party, church and tribe,
his rabble, criminals without a cause.
The dragon burns on.

Margaret Whyte

AWAY WITH IT

Put down that gun you silly man
        And give your neighbour a hand
Help him take care of his family
        Help him take care of the land
Away with aggression . . . Away with war
        Away with hate and prejudice
Look at each other and pleasantly smile
        Don't poison the air with a hiss
Away with bullets . . . Away with bombs
        Away with its howling pain
And all the misery it brings to life
        And the blood that falls like rain
Away with it . . . Away with it
        Wake up and smile and sing
Use philosophy and wisdom
        To make life a wonderful thing
If one cannot help then do not hinder
        Leave each other alone in peace
Work towards coming together
        Or bloody wars will never cease
Away with it . . . Away with it
        Be sensitive to life on this Earth
Inflicting no pain on creature or man
        Throughout each life from birth
Let life be a journey of wonder
        Exhilarating and sweet
So away with it . . . Away with it
        And let happiness dance on your street
Let philosophy and wisdom prevail all the while
        And not the old violent ways
Philosophy and wisdom is the supreme culture
        Heralding soft misty days
When we all can live without fear in our hearts
        Inflicted suffering a thing of the past
Let the bells ring out all over the world

        Peace is here . . . Peace is here at last
I write of my Philosophy and Wisdom
        My Blueprint for civilised peace
Heed my words and live forever by them
        Inflicted suffering then shall cease
Thus Philosophy and Wisdom:
        'Nice words . . . nice thoughts . . . nice attitude . . . nice life'
Philosophy and Wisdom:
        'Try being kind today . . . you never know you may find
        you quite like the experience'
Philosophy and Wisdom:
        'Here's to the last soldier . . . the last crime . . .
        the last injustice'

I'll bid adieu now as I plead in vain
        For human kind to please refrain
From barbarity on animal and on man
        Whilst I do my best . . . the best that I can.

Clare Marie Zeidrah Keirrissia Marshall

WAR

Take away the reasons that man doth turn to war
Take away elitist threats from those who have self-law
Take away possessions that 'what is yours is mine'
Take away the 'he who dares' and those who toe the line
Let us live our normal lives so different from each other
Respecting individual needs that nurture pure Earth Mother
'Tis only then that peace will reign and harmony will sing
At one with all the seasons, from summer through to spring
For just rewards are granted from the maker of this world
As long as time is gentle for the future to unfurl

Lin Bourne

ABSENT HEARTS

Decades past, many years ago, nations fought to conquer
Sacrificed lives were laid beyond the depths of wonder
Shoulder to shoulder in truth and pride, stood dad and lad together.
Defending all they'd left behind, in faith, for freedom ever.

Would that ten million eyes might waken from their sleep
To gaze through hollowed eyes on anniversaries that we keep
Perchance ten million empty crowns, sleeping on pillows of rock
Would turn away in disbelief as at their shrines some mock.

They gave all they had to give on call from Queen and Crown
Now 60 years later they no longer abound
Ultimately in foreign lands they now lie for ever
Empty ships come home alone, many loved ones came home never.

The chill of silent dawn took them where they fell
Echoing the Last Post, to glory - and to Hell
Marching on as they did then with the love from hearts of men
Remember now their gallant valour - remember each of *them*.

Years now of history past, filled so rich and deep
Born of love and gallantry for empty hearts to keep
Point their standards and bugles high, their glory to ever shine
On every anniversary of their sacrifice divine.

F Cooper

A CENTURY OF SHAME

The world resounds with war, threats and lies
and young men die like bloody flies.
Our Jesus' words are drowned by guns
and mothers lose their precious sons.

In a world of hate and fear
we lose a lot that we hold dear.
To talk and bargain, discuss and pray
no one dies to settle wrongs this way.

All countries to be governed by peace alone
words of truth that should be carved in stone.
A hundred years of war and grief
it's senseless, cruel and beyond belief.

Albert Brindle

NO MORE WAR - I PRAY TO GOD

Oh Lord!

Forgive us for our trenchant fear,
That ploughed the fields and scattered sons held dear;
The ingrained manna of our hateful shame
To bury love in graves unmarked of name.

Let future arms be called to bear embrace,
In union, waving flags of one, just race,
Where each surrenders to the greater need,
To plant a softer, kinder-natured seed.

Help us to rise above, like father, like son,
In likewise image once conceived as one;
That we may aim and shoot to long-fought peace,
To grow in light where darkened shadows cease.

Oh Lord! Please aid us from this wicked plight;
Guide us to *all man's land,* no more to fight.
Let cries be heard, for one and all mankind,
In peace that echoes through each distant land;

This prayer of hope that can cast out this day
Hatred's bitter taste -

No more war - I pray!

Ian Deal

THE THINGS ONE SAYS

Not to betray a feeling
That runs - so it seems - too deep
One talks about the state of current affairs
About the unfairness of life
That lets a child die
And no one really knows why
There's so much to blame
So much at stake
So many arguments to be won
To be proven right
No matter what it takes
And we talk as if we know what is right
Without the shadow of a doubt
Yet . . . how can we possibly justify
War, famine, rape?
At this place in time
So much has been achieved
So many wonderful discoveries
The men have been to the moon
Men are getting ready to go to Mars
Yet . . . we are killing our Earth
Our green-blue planet is shrouded in grey
Yet . . . we are the prey
We are killing our children
- If not as casualties of war -
We are killing them emotionally
And then we wonder
At the hostility we see around
When and where along the way
Have we lost our connection to what is real
To that part that knows
There is more to humanity than this?
Yet . . what are we creating
In our own homes?

Who gave us the power to decide
Who lives and who dies?
Why the hate if ultimately
We are the prey of our own game?
What will it take
To look within and truly see
Beyond the pain and further still
To that place where love lives?
Without it life cannot be
Without self-love we are doomed.
All arguments are fearful excuses
If we cannot look within
And honestly ask
'What does one see?'

Celia M Paulo

ATHENA AND PEGASUS

The Roman goddess Minerva
In Greek mythology Athena
The goddess of war arts
Wisdom and crafts
Who had sprung supposedly
From the head of Zeus armed fully
Athens was her chief cult centre
The Parthenon was dedicated to her venture
The winged horse Pegasus
Sprung from the blood of Medusa
In Greek mythology
A constellation in astronomy
Of the northern hemisphere
Clearly assembled to appear
Representing the winged horse Pegasus
Near to Cygnus

Ann Copland

The Misery Of War

The world is lost in turmoil, people blindly travelling round,
Not knowing in which direction, peace of mind and heart is found.
The universe is at boiling point, splitting open at the side,
With misery ruining people's lives, no place where one can hide.

There are the lame, the blind and helpless, it's plain no one understands,
How strange the way of fortune, in bleak and desolate lands.
No one seems to help them, these lost and weary souls,
There surely is an answer, so they reach their peaceful goals.

I pray the Lord will hear them, this lost tormented race,
Who cry out loud for salvation, with no smiles upon their face.
There *must* be a solution and we must ask His aid,
To find it, yes and quickly, for those who cried and prayed.

The soul of this sad nation, with the whole world looking on,
Is begging for help - don't you hear it?
We all need to right what is wrong.
So come Christian men, with the answers, these leaders from
                                                     all round the world,
And give all the help you can muster, your actions speak
                                                     louder than words.

Margaret Warkup

Inhumanity

What is this thing in the human race
deep blood lust rampant in every case?
All religions preach from a moral base
but their peoples act out with frenzied face
they hear the answer in every base
but turn away with blood-stained face
while preaching loud with pious grace.

John E Lindsay

BABI YAR

The grass stands high on Babi Yar.
The trees are softly weeping.
The rustling grass and the bending trees
salute the ones lie sleeping.

No stone is there to mark the spot,
to say who is below.
Just rustling grass and the weeping trees
that's all you need to know.

For if you knew these deathless dead
buried in that ravine
you'd think that they were martyred souls
and keep their memory green.

These men and women committed no crime
so why not give them their due?
A trick of fate had caused them to be
the enemy of the few.

200,000 lie rotting there,
Jews and prisoners of war.
You'll find there the gypsies, the old and the ill
but now they suffer no more.

They stood in the depths of that secret ravine
and faced the German guns.
The sandy rock face of Babi Yar
now covers them from the sun.

The city of Kiev is haunted still
by Babi Yar's renown.
But the only stone that stands to them
is the conscience of that town.

John Clancy

LAMENT FOR A DATE OF BIRTH: THE SACKING OF BERLIN

She is dead
the love my soul had found.

She is dead
and I have just the tales of her decay.

She is gone
and leaves in stone just shadows,
just ideas of ambitions
and the thought that I am late.

She is dead
all laid out for the gloved hands
glass windows - sterility.

She is gone
her rest churned up
from open graves to hollow out my heart.

She is dead
yet cleaved in three the Troika eats itself
and with their own shame bloodied
seek to hand out blame.

She is gone
and lost in smoke between them
I try to follow, want to find but -

She is dead
there's nothing in their graves
just wreckage and regret.

She is gone
and what am I without my trampled trinity?

An uninvited, summoned guest who comes too late
and only sits amidst the rot
too late for

She is dead.

Rebecca Darley

GREYSTOKE

I saw the picture 'Greystoke' and it filled my heart with pain
for though he left the jungle he returned to it again.

Yet Tarzan knew a faithfulness, a love as strong as death -
his 'mother', though a lowly beast, protected with each breath:
she loved her 'bald, adopted son' as though he were her own -
'No matter if he's different, he will not stand alone.'

He suffered at her parting when with arrows she was filled,
for it was men who took her life - their beastly arrows killed;
though they thought him 'uncivilised', man's bloodshed made him sick-
he found and freed his 'father' but again men killed too quick.

The habits of his childhood which were foreign unto men,
came flooding back to comfort as his soul was hurt again.
He owned a large and cheerless house, which didn't mean a thing -
desolate now, he mourned his loss, for what could money bring?

Although he'd left a distant shore to try and live with man,
they'd not enough in common so he had to change his plan.
So man is seen as bestial and beasts are seen as friends,
and Tarzan left the life of ease for one which far transcends.

A pampered life is pointless when there isn't any aim
but Greystoke knew true freedom, when he chose the 'jungle game' -
the family accepted him, were glad to call him Lord,
so with his chosen family he lives in one accord.

Winnie Pat Lee

SILENT TEARS IN OMAGH
PEACE ON EARTH, GOODWILL TO ALL MEN

The North Star shining bright
Above in the sky, of inky velvety blue,
Christmas trees, with twinkling lights,
Children tucked up in bed,
Dreaming of Santa, what will he bring?
Wishing it was dawn
Peace on Earth, goodwill to all men.

Down at the church on the corner
Choir singing, in celebration of
Baby Jesus, born many years ago
On Christmas morn
Peace on Earth, goodwill to all men.

Whilst in a land, not far away
Silently weeping for their great loss
Of children, wives, husbands,
Sisters and brothers,
There will be no Christmas joy,
For the dad who remembers his son
Sat on his knee, as he unwrapped his toys
No future joy, no daughter, to take
Down the aisle of the church
To be married one day, to smile at him
Peace on Earth, goodwill to all men.

No husband to hold the widow's hand,
Or a wife to share his love,
The children's cry for their mother
You cannot have another.
Peace on Earth, goodwill to all men.

In *Omagh*, life will never be the same
For on that dreadful ill-fated day
Loved ones taken from them,
No warning, maimed, murdered,
By men with no conscience, no shame
Pray for *peace, all over the world*
So mankind can walk without fear.
Peace on Earth, goodwill to all men.

Iris Day

CONFUSION

The Bible says 'Thou shalt not kill'
But it seems it's quite OK
To murder in the name of war
As bombs fall day by day.

It really seems so strange to me
That governments decree
That we must fight for justice.
Does killing set us free?

For life is surely precious -
The greatest gift from God.
What right have we to end it?
It really seems so odd.

Yet if a gun were pointed
At my sister, oh so dear,
Would I not rush to save her
Had I a weapon near?

So despite my lofty notions,
Am I a Christian true,
Or a lowly human being
With an unwelcome point of view?

Eileen M Pratt

THE POPPY

The universal symbol of armistice, of soldiers returning,
Of battles ceasing, of wreaths and collecting tins
And November's solemn ceremony.
Its red splash shouts out on postcards,
Impressionist copies, art masters nature.
Painted blobs of vermilion glowing in cornfields,
The paper papaver blooming in June,
Huge cup shapes with their dark, dense dregs
Guarded by straight black fronds of fence,
And then, rain-sodden, the silky cup shape
Flattens into saucers, delicately scalloped
On fat, hairy stalks, raindrops lingering on buds,
Not quite ready to burst into flower.
Green, close, ovate, fat and full of bright red promise.
Innocent and beautiful, enhancing.
Delicate cream, buttercup yellow and deepest peach.
All shades, all sizes in my garden.

On the other side of the world,
Grown to harvest its fruit as a future,
As in trading a cash crop,
To corrupt countless thousands only seeking
To manage life.

Jean Greenall

ASYLUM SEEKERS

Under cover of darkness they came,
silent shadows moving in the purple gloom;
scrambling over rain-filled ditches,
sliding down steep grassy banks
to assault the final hurdle - the wall,
barbed, and razor sharp.

Soaked to the bone, cold, and fearful, they
clawed their way to freedom.
At the mouth of the tunnel the searchlights
picked them off, one by one.
Tonight they would sleep in Sangatte.
Tomorrow, they would try again.

Emelie Buckner

FRAGMENTS OF WAR

I glance with fearful eyes, moving pictures,
Another tragedy in our human vacuum features.

Such pain I do not forget,
It blows in the wind, desert flower dressed in gloomy neglect.
Anguish watches us crying together,
For hatred wears a thick coat of leather,
That usurper of time in this unnamed Earth's place,
I do not know your face . . .

The sun bleeds,
And in every conflict there are silent words,
Masquerading a war clad in veils of nerves, where no one refrains,
Targets to accomplish where only tears serve their gains.
In the distance, from the past, sounds humming the tune of retreat,
A soldier's way to know uncanny feeling of impending defeat.
Relentless bombardment to one's ear spreading the rattle,
Where conference rooms shatter,
This pressure that most of us do not matter.

And all we want, mothers,
To have our sons back, not left to erroneous fate,
For in every warrior rides high the dream of Alexander the Great.

Luisa Allan

GAME OVER

In a world
that's collapsing
under the weight
of rentability.
Invaded casually or
aggressively
by the ravaging sirens
of techno science
the voracity of power
mondialisation.

What remains?

Give me love
and laughter.
Not the cruel
laughter
that comes
of killing as many
fictive characters
as possible
in a   vulgar
          violent
          virtual
          videotape game
never derisive, mocking,
but a laughter born
- of happiness and delight.

Marilyn Hodgson

ULSTER NIGHT OUT

Warmed by rising blue smoke
And tobacco floors,
Noisy chatter fills the bar room.
The soft Irish burr of pleasantries,
Dominoes over a pint of Guinness.

A proud father toasting his son
On his coming wedding day;
About to make a speech,
Suddenly the laughter dies away,
Caught in a shower of exploding glass.

The outer wall; burst its final applause
To the sound of emergency services,
Screeching to a halt. Greeted by screams
'God help us'. Busy hands signing the cross
In the blood and the flesh; and the smoke.

The room spins, a hand grabs my arm
I'm outside somehow, gulping air
Pleading for it all to stop; tears for peace.
Strange voices, ease the sleeping ghosts
Invade my dreams; seep into reality.

400 years of 'bloody fighting'
The same old wounds, that won't heal.
My son's voice, 'Man are you all right'
A glass of Irish whisky in his hand
Helps banish the nightmare.

Jane Bagnall

After The Bomb

Come child and listen to a tale of the past
For now I am old and my memory won't last
Sit by the fire while the candle burns bright
And hear of a world where there was always light

Before the bomb we had beautiful homes
Gardens with flowers, green grass and gnomes
With a touch of a switch brilliant light would appear
Darkness in those days never held fear

People were healthy with skin soft as silk
Plenty of fresh food, vegetables, milk
No one was hungry or sickly like now
How can I possible describe a cow?

You just can't imagine the wonderful land
This country was - now it's barren and bland
Black empty fields with no corn and no wheat
Animals all gone now - nothing to eat

Those of us left have diseases and sores
No hope of a cure now - nothing but wars
Never again will man be what he should
What God intended, healthy and good

History shows that men never learn
Your generation will again take their turn
Wrecking, destruction all over the Earth
Killing, destroying all that has worth

So child, although you may have years of pain
Think of the good things which may come again
If man will stop killing - start building instead
The good Earth will return, not just be in my head.

F Macdonald

BATTLEGROUND

Bombs are falling from the air.
A rain of terror I can't bear.
I see the dead and the dying lying there.
Broken, scattered bodies everywhere.
Cries and screams all around.
As new blasts erupt and shake the riven ground.
I lie cowering behind a broken wall.
My body tight with terror.
Screwed up in a ball.
It's just a broken dream, a nightmare scene, I can see.
This old battleground, it's bunkers and trenches, now buried,
On which less than a century ago,
There lay a sea of bloody mud.
A link to the past; a dreadful racial memory.
They are shades and shadows from the past,
With whom my mind shares a brief empathy.
These ancient memories haunt this scene.
A time ripple in a primeval sea.
This odious, unholy ground.
The dead, unable to sleep safe and sound.
These lost souls wandering aimlessly around.
Their gruesome deaths has left them stranded, earthbound.
Why in all that is Holy; in Heaven's name
Can't this traumatised land be whole again?
Dear God relieve this misery, with your holy light.
Stop this replay, this savage endless fight.
Give these souls, and this soil sweet solace.
Light up this darkness, let this abhorrence cease.
Take these lost ones to Heaven,
Anoint this ill Earth with your holy balm.
Give this poor, grieving landscape peace and calm.

Jonathan Pegg

BALKANS

At their podiums, they announce, with certain confidence pronounce
        with careful timing and script they speak
Our leaders, those of high, exulted office, presumed strength
        in other's eyes, polished veneer, weak

Parties, their ideals, agenda, and with small man's money
        the private games and hidden desires pursued
With cameras, mikes, the actors and their obvious written play
        sound bites, rehearsed bluster, lovingly reviewed

Upon our sets, sleek images, sensual, dark and purposeful machines
        appearance of obvious superiority, obvious control
Trust in us your leaders, what we choose, votes already given
        we're more than you, we have to play our role

Sinister, mean machines, climb with menace into pure and fading blue
        glamorous, shapely, seeming more like sexy fun
Our heroes, years in making, trained, uniformed and unleashed
        evil faceless enemy, start to tremble, start to run

Airy actions on target, with thunder, their frightening carpet song
        replayed at home, distant other worldly drama
Men of brown or green or blue, short words of easy, planned success
        reasons fought in media, fears should be calmer

Objectives still not met, more raids required, again commence
        commanders find their feet, finally fill their roles
Meticulous, precise, years of practise produce such clever plans
        too far removed, no torment will enter their souls

Quick, decisive, incisive action, it's over, so they talk, so they promise
        how history, many times, laughed as others pray
Solid ground from where it starts, quickens, rapidly turns to sand
        sinking steady, new depths each passing a day

Ground, and hearts and minds are never won with painted metal birds
                reserved, our young men, our legions led a slaughter
Sent this familiar, well trodden path, so many have walked before
                not yet quite men, often all too eager for the torture

To see, feel, smell it upon the soil, stark reality, naked, awful, truth
                twisted remains, abstract steel, concrete art of war
Where once may have been a vision, a green and leafy dream
                desolate, silent ruin, in now decorated human gore

Are there things in this life worth fighting for, injustice to rail against
                causes, reasonable beliefs worth dying for
Yes, can live a death in presence of evil, and by dying give others life
                have been times, deserving of the insanity of war

Whoever hailed victorious, lives a state hollow, with which to see
                never real victory, just less suffering in the score
No matter what are social primates say, upon our brightening screens
                all wars paid by the little and powerless, the poor

The pain, the blood, the small family suffering reality, the true loss
                as sticky red seeps beneath each little door
Standing back as far as I am able one question appears to me
                concerns all conflict that in life will ever be, its core

All war is born of failure, no communication, blind myths and beliefs
                no freedom of thought, accept out parents stain
We have learned much, yet so many guns, protect our irrationality
                still without reason do we foster so much pain

Each right of birth is not of choosing, is what's given and must be
                at our end will we wrestle at our heaven's gate
How will we justify our actions, substantiate choices,
                blood on our hands
                as we discover no reason for our hate.

A C Dancer

WHILE YOU STILL HAVE TIME

Dance for me, my pretty,
Fizz like the cola in the bottle
You've just opened,
Smile like the silly drawings
On your party balloons,
All lines curved upwards forever.

While, over there, a girl your age
Sits huddled in ragged misery
By a lonely roadside,
Outside a town as small as this,
Trying not to wonder which gunshot
From inside the mosque
Is the one aimed at her father.

Dance for me, my pretty,
Bounce your new-washed pale hair,
Shining in the radiance
Of you beneath and
The party lights above.

While, over there, a girl your age
Combs from her hair
The brick dust of her missiled home
And wonders where in the rubble
Her mother's body lies.

Dance for me, my pretty,
While the world rages and roars again
In another orgy of blood and tears.

Dance for me, my pretty,
And smile
Before our party ends.

Ted Harriott

OPTIMIST IN RESIDENCE

Optimist in residence was Robert
Muller's unofficial title, earned through
38 years' UN service, keenly
Given in the most campaigning spirit.

Testament to the United Nations,
Robert's farewell book, proclaimed his passion,
Positive approach and love of peace for
All, through constant international effort.

'Organise and institutionalise we
Must as humans,' said he. But the challenge
Was to do it wisely, aiming well for
Love, co-operation, good and welfare.

Chancellor, University for Peace, in
Sunny Costa Rica, was this preacher's
Next position. Prophet-like, he drafted
Ten commandments making outlooks global.

Next came ten for groups and institutions.
These he linked to personal creed and promise.
Three supreme commandments crowned his gospel:
You shall love the Earth and God and others.

We are used for something special on our
Unique planet. If we understand that,
We'll succeed. But if we don't, the cosmos
Something else will try. The choice is ours now.

This was Robert's oft-repeated message,
Dreaming this millennium would be the
First ten hundred years of peace. Such was his
UN wish for our today and future.

Allan Bula

VIETNAM 1965 - A PEASANT'S PLEA

Take my land but leave the soil
Where my roots lie deep untilled.
Rake up the mouldering flesh
But pierce not the cloddèd loam.

My tastes are simple
And my wants are few,
So why embroil me in a
Fight against my kin?

Why shake the sword and
Swirl the dust to canker
Minds to do another's bidding -
When in my heart I have no love of war?

I am goaded on by the *parvenus* of power -
Mere polichinelles of the strategists -
Commandeering tattered worthies, like myself,
To pour their life blood, sweat and guts
Into a cauldron steaming with unrest;
All this, in the name of Peace.

Angela Cheyne

HOLIDAY CAMP?

The sun comes up each morning new
The birds begin to sing
Above the camp in dawn's grey light
The eerie death knells ring

Man's inhumanity to man
Never ceases to astound
The truth of what keeps happening
In genocide is bound

An eye may well be for an eye
And tooth torn out for tooth
Who started it may not be clear
For cycles of doomed youth.

Margo Biggs

SERRE ROAD BRITISH CEMETERY

In this quiet place of green baize lawns
stone regiments geometrically precise
command positions assigned by a cross.
No mud, no blood, no hell
where infantry kept, and still keep
uniformed lines.
Only a sighing of trees
and the murmur of mourners

In fields ripe with old harvests
the rustic scene piles its rusting legacy
of shrapnel shell cases and barbed wire.
The chatter of machine gun
the screams of shell and broken men
only whispers to the few who remember.
And yes, there are token trenches
thick with summer grass - and poppies.

Shattered trees that smouldered
in Delville Wood are in blossom
the scent of flowers lingers
where mustard gas lay in hollows
and a ravaged landscape hides its scars
for the irony of preservation.

Bob Proud

WAR

Benhazi, Tobruck and Alamein,
Battleships, bombs and stuka planes,
Lethal mines and charging tanks,
Shrapnel scything through the ranks,
Desert sands and trucks afire.
Young men dying on the wire.

Battles in the heat of Sicily,
Cassino, Salerno, there in Italy
Cloying mud and freezing rain,
The wounded softly moan in pain,
Cannons roar with hellish noise,
Men soon mature from being boys.

France invaded, soldiers die,
Bombs cascading from the sky,
Paratroops and young marines,
The Devil himself has set the scene,
Belgium, Holland machine guns rattle,
Red berets fall at the Arnhem battle.

Malaya, Burma and jungle green,
An enemy savage, so cruel and mean,
Relentless heat and landing barges,
Swamps, mosquitoes, and 'Banzai' charges,
Mud and sweat, and then monsoon,
From Mandalay to old Rangoon.

All this happened so long ago,
But the youth of today, they don't want to know
As our memories grow dim, and yet
These were the times, *we must never forget.*

William Allan

A PRISONER

Dimming light hems me round. Crushed, after days
Of limb-locked struggle, winter enemies brace
Me to time's wall, to unmake my making.

Breath thins to anguish, pain is my focus;
Dreams are shredded, faith turns to unrhyming dogma.
I am among the dead who colonise the edge of night
And receive no lodging in tomorrow's hope.

Kin to corpses, naked and grimed for the grave,
I hang unseen in an emptiness without guests,
Pinned to lime-washed walls, round, round walls.
Such hurt remains love's question.

Death and its implicit acolyte, unpaid pain, strip my life.
Reliable phantoms scourge, red-swaddle me in flames.
Skin has no reprieve from their ripening plagues.
In this tight fear my tenancy of life nears its close.

Principals in an arcana of cruelty, they twist pain to
Torment, define me for the stress of death. Scars multiply.
No gloss of ease deadens their clasp. Agony patents my life.
I have come to the place where suffering is conceived.

The brilliant nightmare is real, time is torn, the future
Has fled, beauty is effaced in a monotony of dust. I see
Daisy suns no more, nor fly with herons to wind marshes.
Death's dark crawls closer each hour.

Pain swells to an unbearable rack. That I *am*, brings
Their sharpest condemnation. Now, exiled, transfigured to
Night, in ashes of slashed lemon wood, they show me
The withered eyes of children - my child - lining trim graves.

Shall I adjourn the task of words? Can such a psalm be spoken?
Should talk inflect horror, give it symmetry, proportion and rhythm?
Yet not to speak poisons words and fractures the world. So speak . . .

Derek Webster

RECIPES FOR WAR

Where were you when we were starving?
Why didn't the world stop so many dying?
Now violence is the law in our land
After evil men put guns in children's hands

Will your lust for revenge never go?
Why kill someone you don't even know
Just to satisfy a festering desire
To fan cold war ashes into fire?

Why take the land that belonged to me?
You're my countryman yet my worst enemy
Soon from my home I'll be driven outside
To become part of the refugee tide

I'm bred to destroy myself and others
Those who want peace are my hated brothers
I feel joy when I kill and maim
I'm a terrorist brandishing Allah's name

I'm a fighter forced to shelter in Jehovah's birthplace
His message of peace I totally deface
Tanks rattle, guns blast in the stifling heat
None can claim victory, only defeat

Amidst mounting chaos in the world today
Dreams of peace drift further away.

Joyce Atkinson

SEPTEMBER 11TH 2001

It is an ordinary day in September.
Under a pellucid blue sky
workers gather in New York.
They do not know that over the city
planes draw down into its bright towers.
> *Whither shall I go from Thy spirit*
> *Or whither shall I flee from Thy presence?*

The twin towers of commerce
collapse into countless deaths.
Holding briefcases, arms outstretched,
figures fall
like stone crosses
into a death by air
> *If I ascend up into Heaven Thou art there,*
> *If I make my bed in Hell, behold Thou art there*
> *If I take the wings of the morning*

Smoke and ash swell like a black tidal wave
> *And dwell in the uttermost parts of the sea*

People wait with photographs,
hug each other, no longer strangers.
> *Even there shall Thy hand lead me,*
> *And Thy right hand shall hold me.*

Susan Skinner

ISRAEL

Israel why so war torn?

A nation forever forlorn
Each day lives are lost
A battle to everyone's cost
Each day say a little prayer
That someone out there somewhere
Will find a peaceful end
To the war would be a godsend
Why let children be blown up?
Put your ideas in a cup
Stir in the recipe for peace
Only then can the war cease
Let the leaders of the war
Sit down and talk once more
Each other must give an inch
Without a grimace or a flinch
Without that who's land is this
Or that will make them wince
Each has proved they bleed
Here's the real need
Let there be no more greed
So hasten the peace with speed.

F Dyke

EARTH'S HOPE

I see a cross towering above Earth's sorrow
The cross whereon the precious Saviour died.
In this alone lies hope for Earth's tomorrow
Man's only hope is Jesus crucified.

The peace of nations all are vainly seeking
Is found alone in this old rugged cross.
If men would only turn to Jesus' teaching
Soon all which now they seek would seem but dross.

The gentle, pitying Saviour meekly dying
On that cruel cross, yet lives and waits to give
The answer to men's questions, vainly vying
Each one with each to find the way to live.

Oh, nations of the Earth, turn from your seeking
Before it is too late, and come to Jesus' throne
There if you will but listen, you will hear Him speaking
And find all you now seek with that dear loving One.

Joyce Coghlan

SEPTEMBER 11TH

This is spaceship Planet Earth
We're lost in a sea of darkness.
We are trying to reach the light.

This is spaceship Planet Earth
The sun in the east smiled.
When the iron fist in the sky came down
And hit the world's capital.

The child that was never born
Will always speak the loudest
Yet your voice is a whisper that will scar men's hearts.

I know you speak to the winds in your heart.
Did the wind tell you to throw the first stone?

How do you feel tasting the blood
Of a memory that will never learn to speak?
Why did you cry when the winds in your soul began to rain dust?

Why was it so hard for you to learn how to cry?

Don't you understand you have raped an innocent child?

Mark Allibon

WAY OF LIFE

The world I see is like crazy paving
Cracked, uneven, and dirty
Weeds taking over the territory
That doesn't belong to them,
Roots left to spread ugly and clawed
Destroying all in its way,
Countries taking instead of making.

Who are these people who tell us to kill
Because there's a difference in colour and creed?
Why is it so hard for these people to see clearly?
Why do they see the only solution is death?
War is an excuse to take,
War is an excuse to get rid of
And in the middle the innocents
Who know only tears and fear.

Money is no object when war is announced
They find it to kill and to maim,
But ask in the name of peace and you find
That doors are slammed in your face,
War is a way of life now it seems
With peace just a far, distant dream,
But I know in my heart that the day will come
When the wars of this world
Will no longer,
      Reign over us.

Mary Neill

EXODUS

Fleeing the land they were born in.
In their hundreds and thousands they came
Some in carts but mainly on foot,
Like a dark shadow sweeping the plain.

A long twisting road of humanity
The old and the female with young.
Most of the men killed defending their home
Laying dead in a red sinking sun.

Long gaunt faces devoid of all joy,
Eyes mirror their fear and despair.
Rags wrapped around feet too frail for the road
Seeking a refuge somewhere.

Herded like cattle across the land
Penned in a field full of tents.
Transported by buses and railway cars
Not knowing where they're being sent.

Is this what man calls humanity,
To treat their brothers this way?
No, this is called 'ethnic cleansing'
And someone, someday must pay.

We saw it before in the two world wars
And said, 'It won't happen again.'
But Jews or Blacks or Bosnian Serbs
It's happening again just the same.

Elizabeth Brewer

WHY?

I am old, too old to fight
And so I sit here day and night
Listening to my dying land,
Trying so hard to understand.

The reason for this bloody war
That kills the land we loved before,
Is hatred that in small minds grew,
As greed demanded, boundaries new.

Church leaders in Satanic towers
Ignore the suffering that is ours
Their conscience salved by trucks of food,
They bless themselves for doing good.

The authors of this genocide
Insist that God is on their side,
Established churches bless this few,
Is Satan not a Godhead too?

The God who taught the gentle way,
Betrayed by churchmen every day,
The martyrs of Earth's former years
Must look in horror through the tears.

Suffer little children to come unto me,
Not make the children suffer, if with me they'd be
Evil, greed and hatred, are principles today,
Peaceful love and happiness, have long since gone away.

This land I love, is dying slow
Its people have no place to go,
And so we wait with bated breath
The fast approaching hour of death.

Yes I am old, too old to fight,
Yet I must sit here day and night,
Listening to my dying land,
Trying so hard to understand.

Gordon J Hellier

HOLY WAR

Gaping, mouths shout but no ears hear
as bomb-strapped youth stalk rubbled streets
and soldiers swarm beneath a blistering sun.
Their guns are aimed; ready to be fired
when they are goaded by those other boys
some not as old, but desperate as they.
The scene is filled with terror.
Angry mouths are screaming.
Massive tanks are rumbling.
Weeping eyes are bleeding in the deafening array.

Were they ever merely children
playing war games in the sunlight
as we did, back in memory
when boys were Indians and cowboys
protecting territories on autumnal afternoons?

Israelite and Muslim, dispute on Holy acres
that each believed his sanctioned right to own.
Each convinced his cause is just . . . his enemy is wrong
and so hostilities continue
and enraged young tribal warriors
commit unspeakable horrendous acts of war.

Carol Glover

SUBMISSIONS INVITED
SOMETHING FOR EVERYONE

POETRY NOW 2003 - Any subject,
any style, any time.

WOMENSWORDS 2003 - Strictly women,
have your say the female way!

STRONGWORDS 2003 - Warning!
Age restriction, must be between 16-24,
opinionated and have strong views.
(Not for the faint-hearted)

All poems no longer than 30 lines.
Always welcome! No fee!
Cash Prizes to be won!

Mark your envelope (eg *Poetry Now) 2003*
Send to:
Forward Press Ltd
Remus House, Coltsfoot Drive,
Peterborough, PE2 9JX

**OVER £10,000 POETRY PRIZES
TO BE WON!**

Judging will take place in October 2003